SHARED DESTINY

Fifty Years of Soviet-American Relations

*Edited by Mark Garrison
and Abbott Gleason*

*Beacon Press
Boston*

Beacon Press books are published under the auspices
of the Unitarian Universalist Association of
Congregations in North America,
25 Beacon Street, Boston, Massachusetts 02108

Printed in the United States of America

9 8 7 6 5 4 3 2 1

Library of Congress Cataloging in Publication Data

Main entry under title:

Shared destiny.

Includes index.
1. United States—Foreign relations—Soviet Union—
Addresses, essays, lectures.   2. Soviet Union—
Foreign relations—United States—Addresses, essays,
lectures.   I. Garrison, Mark.   II. Gleason, Abbott.
E183.8.S65S54   1985   327.73047   85-47526
ISBN 0-8070-0200-3

SHARED DESTINY

To future generations of American sovietologists, whose work on both American and Soviet attitudes is cut out for them

The Center for Foreign Policy Development promotes research and discussion on U.S. policy for dealing with the Soviet Union. It brings together scholars from various disciplines and present or former practitioners in the executive and legislative branches of government. Their thinking is leavened when possible by engaging interested persons from public interest organizations, journalism, and politics and by taking account of public opinion. The objective is to develop policy ideas for the future which are well founded in scholarship and experience and are at the same time easily accessible to citizens and politicians. The Center was founded in 1981 and incorporated in 1982 as a nonpartisan, nonprofit research institution. Logistics are provided by Brown University, where it is located. It is funded by grants from private individuals and foundations.

CONTENTS

PREFACE

The fiftieth anniversary of the formal beginning of a
relationship—personal or diplomatic—is an appropriate
time for retrospection. In the case of the lectures that
gave birth to this book, however, the felt need for a re-
appraisal of U.S.-Soviet relations came first. The fortu-
itous fact that the timing fell on the fiftieth anniversary
of the formal establishment of diplomatic ties was a coin-
cidence that lent poignancy and weight to the lectures.

The four lectures delivered in Providence, Rhode
Island, during October and November 1983 resulted
from a collaboration among the World Affairs Council
of Rhode Island, the Center for Foreign Policy Development at Brown University, and members of the Brown
University faculty. The lectures were organized in response to a shared perception that relations between the
two superpowers had become so dangerous that it was
imperative to take stock of the problem, of how it had
evolved, and how it might be handled in the future.

Following an introduction by Abbott Gleason demonstrating that some aspects of U.S.-Soviet relations have roots in Russo-American relations in the nineteenth and early twentieth centuries, those four lectures form the nucleus of this book. George Kennan—who not only took part in establishing the first American embassy in Moscow but was also an architect of postwar U.S. policy toward the Soviet Union—offers insights from a lifetime spent on the study of that country. John Lewis Gaddis comments from the perspective of a historian who has exhaustively analyzed the containment policy that Kennan inspired. Adam B. Ulam examines specific cases of U.S.-Soviet interaction in order to draw conclusions about the communication problem between the two societies. Alexander Dallin criticizes American attitudes and the fallacies that he believes underlie them.

Two other distinguished scholars agreed to contribute chapters that add important psychological and perceptual dimensions: Robert Dallek finds the roots of American attitudes toward the Soviet Union in our own domestic concerns; Hans Rogger, reviewing Russian and Soviet perceptions of the United States from the early nineteenth century until 1984, suggests how powerful are the continuities on the Russian-Soviet side. The volume concludes with an afterword by Mark Garrison that posits that the nuclear weapons policies of the two countries have diminished the security of both.

A Soviet scholar was scheduled to deliver a lecture in the 1983 series in order to provide a Soviet perspective on the first fifty years of U.S.-Soviet relations. That lecture would have been included in this volume, but his trip to the United States was canceled in the wake of the shooting down of the Korean Air Lines passenger aircraft. The event put a tragic point on the dangerous realities of U.S.-Soviet relations. One incidental result was that this book became a purely American effort to look back and understand the relationship, and to fathom the reasons for both American and Soviet behavior. Perhaps that is as it should be, for it brings home that the Soviet side would also be well advised to go over the same ground, through Soviet eyes and sensibilities, searching for the reasons for both countries' attitudes. Each side would then be better equipped to deal with the reality that both are the enemies of each.

In putting together this volume we have incurred significant debts that we acknowledge with gratitude. To Thomas J. Watson, Jr., we are indebted not only for suffusing our efforts with his deep concern about the importance of U.S.-Soviet relations, but also for his active help on this project, without which key elements would not have fallen into place. We are deeply grateful to Leonard Cohen, of the World Affairs Council of Rhode Island, for his collaboration in conceiving and presenting the lectures, and to the Rhode Island Committee on the Humanities and Carl W. Haffenreffer for financial support which helped make the lecture series possible. We are indebted to Dan Caldwell for the suggestion that the series be focused on the fiftieth anniversary of the establishment of relations. And the volume would not have been possible without the wisdom and eloquence of the contributors, as well as their patience in abiding our ministrations.

INTRODUCTION

Abbott Gleason

From the vantage point of late 1984, Orwell's year, it is easy to find oneself thinking of all the utopias and dystopias that the European world has produced, so many of them looking to the late twentieth century. Many, if not the majority, suggested—in hope, sorrow, or terror—that by this time the nations, cultures, and regions of the world would be growing more and more alike. Totalitarianism, the global village, socialism or communism, modernization are all at bottom versions of a convergence theory. And of course there *has* been some convergence, and no doubt there will be more. Greeks in a remote village jam the local bistro to watch "I Love Lucy" on their national television. The Iranian Revolution (or counter-revolution—it is characteristic of 1984 that we are not sure which it is) was technically dependent on the same kind of tape cassettes on which my children depend. Increasingly it is British popular culture that creates the vocabulary for the adolescent rebellions of the world.

There is a McDonald's on the Champs Elysée. Jeans are still as sought after in the Soviet Union as in years past; the newest fad is jogging shoes, known there as *keddy* (older readers will remember when U.S. Keds were a major American sneaker). Soviet leaders are powerless to do anything about this particularly odious cosmopolitanism.

But these convergences are superficial. These days the world's nations treasure their differences, not their similarities. Archaic national or cultural identities become more, not less, important with each passing day. Fundamentalism has already changed the political and social face of the Islamic world. The situation is not utterly dissimilar in Israel. And in the United States and the Soviet Union, to whose rather discordant relationship this volume is devoted, powerful currents of nationalism and traditionalism may also be felt. Perhaps the power and ubiquity of this nativism in the world today have affected the distinguished and diverse contributors to this volume, for in spite of major ideological and geopolitical reasons for the rivalry between the United States and the Soviet Union, one finishes reading these essays with a deep sense of the importance of divergent cultures and histories in producing the dangerous situation in which we currently find ourselves. "We have met the enemy and he is us," said Walt Kelly's Pogo. Americans like that idea less and less these days; even when they find virtue in it, what it suggests they should do is not clear. In Russia's cultural context, such a notion is absurd, subversive, or both—perhaps because it activates a deep and old fear. There is an old Russian peasant proverb: *Ne vynesti sora iz izby* (Don't sweep the litter out of the hut), meaning something close to the American adage about not washing your dirty linen in public. While Americans have come to glory in the public washing of dirty linen, the experience of Russian peasant culture powerfully suggests how dangerous it is to reveal division or weakness of any kind to the enemy, or perhaps even to oneself.[1]

One of the dimensions of the essays in this volume, explicit or implicit, is that both sides need to take each other seriously in the other's terms. To take others seriously does not, of course, mean to give in to them, although occasionally this confusion has plagued American students of Russia in the native political context. It does entail a strenuous and steady effort vicariously to enter the Russians' world, to understand their history, to learn how they talk—not merely the forms of their language, but what they mean by what they say. If both sides could decide that this dangerous world necessitates such an effort, the danger would begin to lessen. But the current hostility increases cultural isolationism and the retreat into strength.

The relatively new (from the historian's point of view) subject of Soviet-American relations is embedded in and the outgrowth of the older subject of Russian-American relations. Between 1780 and 1880, this relationship was not very important for either side, which helps explain its relative harmoniousness. To American statesmen of the late eighteenth and early nineteenth centuries, the political and social point of view of the Russian autocracy was largely repulsive, but no one was minded to call for a crusade, the United States then being a champion of nonintervention across the Atlantic. In a practical way, the fact that both the United States and Russia tended to be anti-British was far more important than political or philosophical differences about the proper organization of society; and this common hostility often fostered at least lukewarm relations. During the American Civil War, the government of the Union was grateful for Russian support, which paved the way for the sale of Alaska, but no image of Russia had been broadly and deeply established in American public opinion.

In the last third of the nineteenth century, particularly after 1881, the tepid cordiality between Russians and Americans at the official level began to show signs of strain. The problems that led to the downturn in relations between Imperial Russia and the United States of America play almost as central a role today. The cluster of issues centers on how the Russian (or Soviet) government treats its own people, especially political dissenters and non-Russians. If they are badly treated, is it the business of the United States to improve their situation? If it is the business of the United States to work for the betterment of those living under the Russian scepter, how is one to do it? Should the United States offer economic inducements to Russians if they do treat certain categories of people better? Should it penalize them if they do not? John Gaddis suggests that American leverage, in matters pertaining to Russian political institutions or political culture, has been weak.[2]

The initial focus of the discussions on whether the United States can make life better for people living in Russia, which have proceeded episodically for more than a century, was the position of Jews in Russia. In 1881, after the assassination of Alexander II, the "Tsar Liberator," pogroms broke out in more than one hundred localities in Russia; according to a reliable recent account, these anti-Semitic outbreaks were the most dreadful and widespread of the century.[3] The great wave of East European Jewish emigration to the United States had begun before the pogroms, but they certainly lent it force; by 1914, the Jewish population of the United States had grown to about three million, ten times what it was in 1880.[4]

One result of this massive emigration was that the question of American attitudes toward Russia's discrimination against its Jewish population was—for the last thirty-five or forty years of the Imperial regime—entangled with the fate of Jews who were born under the Russian scepter but who had found their way to the United States. Many American business firms, for instance, entrusted their interests in Russia to American citizens who were born in Russia (often Jews) but who had emigrated to the United States. Since emigration from Russia without special permission (very difficult to obtain) was illegal under Russian law, when such people returned to Russia to represent American firms, see about personal affairs, or visit family, they were often harassed, expelled, or even arrested. Already in the 1870s American diplomats in Russia were discovering that the difficulties of naturalized Americans of Jewish origin were taking up a surprisingly large percentage of their time.[5] As early as 1873, Hamilton Fish, the American Secretary of State, had felt it necessary to lodge a vigorous protest in St. Petersburg. For the last thirty years of the nineteenth century, American consciousness of how the Russian government persecuted its Jewish population was kept high by the awareness of the difficulties of American Jews in Russia. Even Jews who were not of East European origin were usually treated not as Americans but as Jews and were entangled in the increasingly complex web of discriminatory legislation that defined and governed the lives of Russian Jews.

As is well known, the situation of Russian Jews deteriorated after 1881, due to an increasingly chauvinist point of view emanating from official circles and to a set of policies devoted to cultural and political russification of the Russian Empire's minorities. Indeed, though the evidence is sketchy, it may well be that the anti-Russian shift in American public opinion, so marked in the last quarter of the nineteenth century, owes even more to those policies than is commonly realized, for the Polish, Finnish, and Baltic immigrants to the United States also brought with them a virulently anti-Russian point of view, which had not been nearly so pronounced in earlier waves of immigration. And as the American mass media and public opinion developed, such issues had an increasing resonance within American society.

After the assassination of Alexander II in 1881, Russian officials seem to have become increasingly convinced that in addition to their "oriental" natures and "parasitical" way of life, Jews were also likely to become "nihilists," adducing as evidence the (scarcely surprising) fact that Jews were well represented in the ranks of the Russian revolutionary movement. In the late 1880s, Jewish access to higher education was further restricted. In 1891, with the formidable russifier Ivan Durnovo installed as Minister of the Interior and the Emperor's brother, the Grand Duke Sergei, as Governor-General of Moscow. the categories of Jews permitted to live outside the Pale of Settlement[6] were suddenly reduced, resulting in large numbers of Jews being uprooted from Moscow, St. Petersburg, Kharkov, and other cities—an estimated twenty thousand from Moscow alone.[7]

The events of the next twelve or fifteen years saw an even further growth of hostility toward Russia in American public opinion, as russification policies became increasingly systematic and widespread, and emigrants from the Russian Empire continued to land on American shores.[8] But after the turn of the century, a more practical set of disagreements was added to and blended with the growing resentment on both sides about ethnic issues. With China almost completely helpless, the clash of rival imperialisms in the Far East was becoming a bitterly contested and nasty conflict, helping to realign the European and the world order, putting new kinds of pressures on apparently stable relationships, and bringing about strange bedfellows, on occasion in whirlwind fashion. England, the United States, Russia, and Japan were among the most deeply involved in China, especially in the struggle to control Manchuria and achieve a dominant position in the railroad building going on across the Far East. The United States enthusiastically supported Japan in its war with Russia (American bankers provided major loans to Japan), in the belief that Russia represented the major danger to America's Open Door policy (rough equality of opportunity for the imperial powers in China). At least one extremely important American banker, Jacob Schiff of Kuhn, Loeb, supported Japan financially in part because of Russian anti-Semitism. But following the

Russo-Japanese War, the Russians and the Japanese found it more expedient to divide Manchuria between them than to acquiesce in the not very adroit efforts of the United States to keep the door open. Imperial rivalries did as much to sour Russian-American relations in some quarters as Russian chauvinism and racism did in others. The Russians, by contrast, were only interested in American racism as a rhetorical means of retaliating against American attacks.[9]

A final strand in the deterioration of relations between 1890 and 1917 was the discovery and dramatization of the Russian system of exiling political prisoners to Siberia. In the famine year of 1891, within a few months of the highly publicized expulsion of Jews from Moscow and St. Petersburg, an American journalist named George Kennan (the great-uncle of the distinguished diplomat-historian who has contributed to this volume) published a large collection of the increasingly successful lectures he had been giving across the United States over the previous several years. The publication of Kennan's *Siberia and the Exile System* inaugurated what will soon be a full century of American interest in and sympathy for Russian political prisoners, which has much in common with our defense of Russian Jewry. Lobbies with titles like "The Friends of Russian Freedom" began to make their appearance at the end of the 1890s and have become a familiar feature of the Russian-American relationship over long periods of time. How much good has been accomplished by such organizations is harder to establish.

An early climax in the downhill course of relations in the early twentieth century came with the infamous pogrom at Kishinev (the capital of Bessarabia) in 1903, in the course of which more than one hundred Jews were seriously injured or killed, some five hundred were hurt, and thousands were rendered homeless. The operations of the Russian legal system added insult to injury. Only a few of the rioters received even light sentences, and the Russian ambassador in Washington issued a repellent anti-Jewish statement, implying that the victims were guilty of exploiting their Russian neighbors and virtually deserved what they got. Indignation was widespread in the United States; protest meetings were held all over the country, and public opinion was much inflamed.[10]

In addition to the damage done to Russian-American relations, the massacre led to the founding of the American Jewish Committee in 1906, thus adding a sophisticated and well-connected group of participants to the anti-Russian lobbying in Washington, now steadily increasing in intensity and effectiveness. Focusing on the demand that Russia treat all holders of American passports equally, the American Jewish Committee helped keep the issue of Russian anti-Semitism before both Republicans and Democrats in the election of 1908. The committee went on to play an important role in the campaign that ultimately forced President Taft to abrogate the Russian-American Commercial Treaty of 1832, on the grounds that Russia continued to violate it by discriminating against Americans because of their religious beliefs. The cause became national in 1911, and by the end of the year overwhelming majorities in both houses of Congress forced the president to abrogate.

A number of Russians in official positions, observers in Western Europe, and some American critics of abrogation pointed out the anomalies. The United States was probably as rich in racisms as Russia, though their expression may have been less intense. The number of blacks lynched per year was high; blacks had been disenfranchised in the South, and Chinese exclusion laws were being passed. Nor was the country free from anti-Semitism. None of these circumstances had any very marked effect, either in mitigating the criticism of Russia or in diminishing the power of racism in this country.

The response of Tsarist Russia to the abrogation of the 1832 trade treaty should not be completely surprising to someone familiar with the Jackson-Vanik Amendment and other efforts to pry a commitment to substantial and regular Jewish emigration from the Soviet Union in the 1970s. Nationalist elements in the Duma were strengthened by the wave of anger that swept the Right and Center of Russian public opinion. The influential daily newspaper *Novoe vremia* (New Times) wrote that the whole affair demonstrated the degree to which "Jewish bankers have become the real lords of America," and the paper angrily remarked that only if Miliukov (the Anglophile historian who led the liberal Kadet Party) became prime minister would the Americans get the concessions they demanded.[11] Ranks were often closed to a greater than usual degree when the Right could evoke the prospect—in this case the fait accompli—of *outsiders* telling Russians how to manage their affairs. The Russian government, still publicly courteous, explained again to the American government that it could not allow Jewish nihilists to enter Russia freely without putting its very existence in jeopardy.[12] It again took note of the fact that Russian citizens of Mongolian birth could not be admitted to the United States, so the Americans were clearly not opposed to all such racial exclusion. Since the Americans were not acting out of principle, the real cause had to lie in the pandering of American politicians to Jewish voters. The American Jewish Committee and other Jewish organizations were influential, of course, and so was the presence of a large Jewish electorate in such states as New York and Massachusetts, but the crudeness and simplicity of the Russian charges suggest how poorly the Russians understood the mix of genuine idealism, pragmatism, and lack of a felt need for consistency that characterized American political culture.

Despite some doubters and cynics, the initial American response was often euphoric and patriotic. The cartoonist Macauley in the New York World depicted a stern American eagle, dressed in an Uncle Sam suit, defeating an incredulous Russian bear at checkers. The American press was virtually unanimous in hailing the abrogation, with liberal, socialist, and Jewish journals especially fervent in their praise.[13]

But after all was said and done, the position of Jews in Russia was in no way improved by the American action; indeed in the short run it deteriorated. American Jews traveling to Russia found no alteration in their legal situation. Russian-American relations were in small ways briefly damaged by the affair, but not seriously, since those interests devoted to trade in both countries found a way to achieve their ends. During the First World War, ill feeling receded on both sides, with so many more momentous things to think about.

From this distance, certain aspects of these disputes may be worth some thought. Both sides adhered to points of view that had deep roots in their respective cultures. Both revealed profound insularities. In a sense, none of the policy issues considered normal or customary at the time were at issue: unconnected to any larger policy considerations, the United States was in effect insisting publicly that Russia cease to be anti-Semitic or face rather trifling economic difficulties. Russia of course refused. Although neither side yielded, it is worth observing how the behavior of each confounded the other. The Imperial Russian government was astonished that the American government would go to such lengths over the plight of "a few Jews." The American public and Congress (if not American diplomats) were apparently surprised that the Russians would not yield on this issue for even the rather measly economic stakes. And they were further disappointed when no European state followed the American example of going to economic sanctions. It had thus been suggested for the first time how difficult it might be for a campaign of public pressure to force the Russians to make concessions on how they treated non-Russians, but how popular such a campaign might become within the United States. And the *New York Evening World* suggested that American abrogation of the Treaty of 1832 implied the repeal of our Chinese Exclusion Law, for surely after such a campaign we would exclude no immigrants on the grounds of race alone.[14] In a culture in which the polarity of ours and theirs, native and alien was so sharply defined, such conflicts were likely to result in an improved situation for Russian Jews only under unusual circumstances, as they briefly did during the 1970s.

The 1917 revolution brought other issues to the fore, as well as other persons. American diplomacy and public opinion were long concerned with such practical matters as the Soviet refusal to pay the claims against, and the debts of, the Tsarist government; there were also the even more significant ideological issues: Soviet attempts to foment revolution worldwide, whether in support of a genuinely revolutionary point of view or (as increasingly came to be believed) in support of something closer to old-fashioned imperial interests. These were the issues that impeded American recognition of the Soviet Union and with which Franklin Roosevelt had to deal in 1933.

It is extraordinarily difficult to make even a provisional separation of ideological, geopolitical, and military issues from those that have their roots in the deeper reaches of the culture, although many have tried. For a time it truly appeared—and not just to hopeful leftists—that whatever the errors or brutalities of Soviet communism, it had at least made anti-Semitism in the Russian traditional style into something vestigial. But it is striking indeed how, since World War II, older and more "Russian" elements have come to the fore in Soviet culture, which has come to resemble markedly—in its patriotism, chauvinism, and general premodernism—the Imperial Russia of the last two tsars. It is in this situation that the Soviet-American dialogue of the last fifteen years or so has come to approximate more closely the older Russian-American dialogue and to embody older cultural oppositions more fully.

It is not plausible to assume that Americans will soon give up their concern for religious or ethnic minorities in the Soviet Union—nor, in my opinion, should they. Part of our sense of ourselves as a nation is that we *are* concerned about the fate of powerless people far away; such concerns make us in most ways better people, if not as good as we sometimes believe or are told. And we are a nation of emigrants, all of whom came from somewhere else. But given the balance of terror in the world and the importance of our dialogue with Soviet Russians, perhaps it is not too much to hope that we may become less quixotic and extravagant in our aspirations to do good, that all of us may realize that, to be effective, such aspirations must be disciplined and made part of a coherent policy.

Whether those who make Soviet policy can learn that American efforts on behalf of faraway people are not just a blend of hypocrisy and cynicism remains to be seen.[15] In any event, it is more vital with every passing month that we understand how to talk to them, and they to us. Such an understanding is more important than it was in the 1970s and incomparably more important than at the end of 1911.

Adam Ulam's essay directly addresses the problem of how to talk and listen to each other. In speaking of the necessity for better communication between the United States and the Soviet Union, Ulam is not merely suggesting greater analytical care and a longer attention span but also implying that the relationship between rhetoric and reality on both sides is not what it appears to be. Implicit in what he says is the undeniable fact that both the United States and the Soviet Union speak in profoundly national accents, and if representatives of one side perceive only the constant muddy rhetorical stream of the other, opportunities for fruitful discussion can appear and then disappear.

Both Alexander Dallin and John Gaddis are concerned with patterns of behavior and interaction that have, for better or for worse, proved durable. It is ironical that, as Dallin writes, both the Soviet Union and the United States have a tendency to see their conflict in heavily ideological and doctrinaire terms; for different reasons, both sides are locked into such vocabularies. A more traditional "great power" view of the relationship has been gaining some ground in recent years, but as so often happens when relations deteriorate, ideological interpretations become more powerful and all-encompassing. Apart from the analytical usefulness of a great power point of view of superpower relations, to the extent that each is able to view the other in that framework, it allows greater scope for negotiation and accommodation and diminishes essentialist differences that are not really negotiable. It is also Dallin's conviction that the United States has a clear tradition of overideologizing its relationship with the Soviet Union, on occasion by seeing regional economic and political problems as made in Moscow or by acting as if the essential problem were not one of a global but external challenge from the Soviet Union, but one of domestic Communist subversion.

Dallin shares with John Gaddis (and Adam Ulam) the conviction that the challenge presented to the United States by the Soviet Union is at bottom traditional. Such a conclusion implies that the traditional means of diplomacy are essential for both sides and that the history of great-power relations is a useful study, however unprecedented the destructive means now possessed by both sides. Gaddis's analysis is particularly free from reference to ideology. He sees the heart of the Soviet challenge to the United States in the sort of linkage between great power and "great insecurity" that has often been observed by students of Russia interested in political culture and disposed to believe in the shaping power of historical experience.[16] Gaddis regards the apparent Soviet conviction that their "security interests require the indefinite expansion of [their] influence at the expense of the security interests of others" as the most essential problem facing American policy-makers, although he takes note of the fact that the manner in which we linked our own security to the survival of the South Vietnamese regime suggests that we are not immune to the same tendency. Gaddis also stresses the degree to which our experience suggests that the Soviet Union almost never responds to unilateral gestures, but to countervailing power, wielded not provocatively or in such a way as to challenge their safety or legitimacy, but sufficient for the existing challenge.

All the scholars in this volume deplore the tendency of American policy-makers to project domestic problems, fears, and aspirations on the world of foreign relations, but Robert Dallek makes this charge a central part of his vigorous criticism of the American style of foreign-policy making, in particular when that policy is toward the Soviet Union. A "Soviet state," he writes, "which was so at odds with American institutions and beliefs intensified American fears about the state of the nation." At the end of both world wars and at present, the United States has engaged in a good deal of internal controversy about values, and it has been easy for conservatives to link the struggle against left-wing values at home with the struggle against the Soviet Union, whose espionage activities in the United States strengthen the plausibility of assertions that the hidden hand of Moscow is linked to the subversive activities of liberals or leftists at home. During World War II, a time when geopolitical realities dictated good relations between the U.S. and the U.S.S.R., Americans had to persuade themselves, by contrast, that Soviet citizens were becoming much like us. The conclusion seems inescapable: Americans still need to understand that great powers—let alone global powers—cannot afford to have relations only with nations whose values are like their own, with what we call friends, nor can all their allies be congenial. We can and must have relations with some extremely unfriendly and nasty regimes; and we ought to discipline our tendency either to deny their nastiness or to feel that if their culture is inimical to ours we must be enemies across the board.

If it is plausible to argue that American attitudes

toward Russia and the Soviet Union can be attributed in some part to an externalization of American anxieties and cultural biases, it should also be pointed out that Russian and Soviet views of America have been complexly tailored to fit the internal dramas of Russian culture. At the end of the eighteenth century and for much of the nineteenth, the United States was a symbol, in the political and cultural world of Russia, of radical extremism. It was the spawn of the Enlightenment; it was the living negation of the slogan of the Russian emperor Nicholas I: "Orthodoxy, Autocracy, and Nationality." As Russia developed an intransigent Left in the course of the nineteenth century, its partisans naturally interested themselves to some degree in America—above all how it worked and (for they were Russian intellectuals) what it meant. As bitter left-wing opponents of the Russian autocracy, many of them were attracted by the libertarian American experiment; and some, out of curiosity or ideological sympathy, even traveled here.[17]

But for a number of reasons, there were always rather narrow limits to the attractiveness of the United States to Russian radicals. For on the whole, the values of the Russian Left were communal and socialist—and nationalist, too, in their romantic love of Russia and obsession with its destiny. To such leftists, the American scene often seemed appallingly materialistic and individualistic —a cruel, bleak Darwinian landscape where violence and hucksterism prevailed. Everything in America was for sale. The Americans might be politically the freest people in the world, but when Russian intellectuals saw what the Americans were doing with political freedom, many were reinforced in their belief that a revolution that cleared the way for such a rapacious capitalism was the wrong revolution, if indeed it was one at all. Russian radicals preferred to dream much more apocalyptic dreams of the total regeneration of Russia, or all of Europe, or even of humanity, through the collective institutions and spirit of the Russian peasantry which would come to the fore in the *Russian* Revolution, which these nineteenth-century men and women correctly foresaw as being very different from the American one. Conservative and romantic intellectuals such as Fedor Dostoevsky were even more hostile to American values. They shared the romantic communalism of the Left but were not in the least attracted by the commercial dynamism of the Americans, their productivity, or their economic individualism, as the radicals might be to some degree.

One can begin to understand this hostility toward America by taking note of what an agrarian society Russia was until well after the revolution of 1917, of how agrarian and antibourgeois its values were. Neither the subsistence agriculture of the Russian village nor the social existence of the Russian landed gentry, who as a group were notably unsuccessful at putting their estates on a "scientific," moneymaking footing, was very hospitable to economic individualism, whose successes often appeared to be speculation and whose best exemplars often bore foreign names. The Russian commercial middle class was weak and late in developing, and it got almost no respect from groups that were socially dominant at least in the sense that they bequeathed many of their values to Russian political culture in the twentieth century: the aristocracy, the radical intelligentsia, and above all the peasantry. None of them were successfully oriented to making money; if they began to do so, their achievement might be greeted with a special hostility, as well as envy. The landed aristocracy was unable as a group to respond to the emerging market economy after the emancipation of the serfs. The Russian village remained poor, isolated, and backward during the same period. A scattered group of peasants did prosper after 1861; they were called kulaks (fists), the old Russian peasant term for rich neighbors, now known to much of the outside world thanks to Stalin's "liquidation" of them in the 1930s.

Many Americans with some exposure to Russian history—a college course, perhaps—know roughly what a kulak is and (without subscribing to dekulakization) that kulaks are "bad." But if you described the same peasant to them without calling him a kulak, stressing how hard he worked, how he went without grain this year in order that his harvest next year should be greater, how hard he drove others (but most of all himself), how practical (pragmatic) he was, how he felt that his worldly success entitled him to special respect and deference in his community, they might realize how culturally relative a negative valuation of the kulak is. A powerfully pejorative term in Russian culture, but in the American context? We are kulaks here, many of us, or the sons and daughters of kulaks. America was in crucial ways made (for better or for worse) by kulaks. One might also suggest that Ronald Reagan aspires to be a kulak president. Much of American culture—especially its more archaic aspects —is rather akin to points of view that would have been called kulak in a Russian context, however far from such a position the high culture of American intellectuals may have become. In Russia, it was generally assumed that the kulak's success came at the expense of the rest of the population. In America, the success and influence of the enterprising were not believed to have deleterious consequences for everybody else.

Of course, the Russian view of the United States was in actuality broader, fuzzier, and more ambivalent than the antikulak caricature I have sketched out. Russians did admire the drive and energy of American civilization: the rationalism, the antitraditionalism, the sense of building a new world, the ability to get things done, and the display of power. The acquisition of those qualities, after all, was part of Peter the Great's program for Russia and close to the original sense of Europeanization to which even the Romanov dynasty remained committed, at least in theory, until the reign of the last tsar. On occasion, one even found Russians linking these Promethean attributes and referring to them collectively as *Amerika-*

nizm.[18] But communal and collective values were so powerful throughout Russian culture, albeit in rather different ways among the upper than in the lower classes, that it was difficult for a prerevolutionary Russian to admire *Amerikanizm* without major reservations. Hans Rogger, more than any other scholar, has defined over the years the cultural continuities from the Russian view of America to the Soviet, and it was natural for the editors to ask him to undertake a synthesis for this volume.

George Kennan's essay, which recounts the obstacles to understanding he encountered in both countries, is especially poignant because he devoted a substantial portion of his life to Soviet-American relations. For experienced students of our somber subject, his essay will evoke a great deal of color, atmosphere, and feeling, no less than of issues. To newcomers to the subject, it should say something about the cultural as well as political distance that separates even the most brilliant and sensitive Americans from Russia.

This brings us full circle. George Kennan's essay also reminds us that we have a duty to remember that we and the Russians share a common humanity, even as we commit ourselves never fatuously to deny how different we are. His evocative sketch will recall to us the necessity of continuing efforts at self-understanding, even as we try to understand the other, and that a sense of irony and humility are priceless attributes for the American student of the Soviet Union.

NOTES

1. I owe the quotation to Edward Keenan's thought-provoking unpublished paper, "Russian Political Culture," especially pp. 13–21. See also the discussion that follows.
2. In addition to the essay in this volume, see his introduction to the subject in *Russia, the Soviet Union and the United States: An Interpretive History* (New York, 1978), pp. 28–32.

3. Ann E. Healy, "Tsarist Anti-Semitism and Russian-American Relations," *Slavic Review*, Vol. 42, No. 3 (Fall 1983), p. 408.

4. Healy, "Tsarist Anti-Semitism," pp. 408–409.

5. Browsing through the relevant volumes of the official documents on American foreign relations suggests the importance of the issue. See, for example, "Russia," *Papers Relating to the Foreign Relations of the United States, Transmitted to Congress . . . December 5, 1881* (Washington, D.C., 1882), pp. 991–1041.

6. The "Pale of Settlement": those western portions of the Russian Empire in which Jews were permitted to reside after the Partitions of Poland in the late eighteenth century vastly increased Russia's Jewish population.

7. Significantly, these unpleasant policies attracted sufficient attention in the United States to draw the censure of President Harrison in his message to Congress in 1891. Nevertheless, American philanthropy provided Russia with considerable relief during the serious famine of 1891. But with public opinion turning increasingly against Russia, government participation in the relief effort proved unfeasible. Congressman Pendleton of West Virginia proclaimed that "friendship between tyranny and liberty; between Asiatic despotism and modern civilization; between the inertia of barbarism and the spirit of progress" was impossible—rather, modern-sounding language in the Russian-American dialogue. See William Orbach, *The American Movement to Aid Soviet Jews* (Amherst, 1979), p. 118.

8. See, inter alia, Archibald Carey Coolidge, *The United States As a World Power*, New York, 1908, pp. 217–220; Thomas A. Bailey, *America Faces Russia: Russian-American Relations from Early Times to Our Day* (Ithaca, 1950), pp. 169–171.

9. See Boris A. Romanov, *Rossiia v. Manchzurii, 1892–1906*, Leningrad, 1928; Edward H. Zabriskie's excellent *American-Russian Rivalry in the Far East*, London, 1946; V. V. Lebedev's *Russko-Amerikanskie ekonomicheskie otnosheniia (1900–1917)*, Moscow, 1964, pp. 18–145; and the fine summary treatment by John Gaddis in his *Russia, the Soviet Union and the United States* (New York, 1978), pp. 32–56.

10. See Hans Rogger, "Tsarist Policy on Jewish Emigration," *Soviet Jewish Affairs*, Vol. 3, No. 1, 1973, 26–37; Isidore Singer, *Russia at the Bar of the American People*, New York, 1904; Cyrus Adler, *The Voice of America on Kishineff* (Philadelphia, 1904).

11. Translation from the *Literary Digest*, December 30, 1911, p. 1214.

12. See Sazonov's conversation with the American ambassador, reported in *Papers Relating to the Foreign Relations of the United States* (Washington, D.C., 1918), pp. 696–698.

13. See *Literary Digest*, December 30, 1911, Vol. 63, pp. 1213–1214; Bailey, *America Faces Russia*, pp. 220–223; Max Kohler, "The Abrogation of the Treaty of 1832 between the United States and Russia and the International Protection of Religious Minorities" in Luigi Luzzatti, *God in Freedom* (New York, 1930), pp. 729–734.

14. *Literary Digest*, December 30, 1911, p. 1215.

15. A recent Soviet book conveys some grounds for pessimism. In discussing the deterioration of Russian-American relations in the period we have been discussing, the Soviet historians N. V. Sivachev and N. N. Yakovlev simply do not take American concern about Russian Jews seriously. See their *Russia and the United States* (Chicago, 1979), pp. 18–24.

16. A classic of such analysis is Louis J. Halle, *The Cold War As History* (New York, 1967).

17. See David Hecht, *Russian Radicals Look to America, 1825–1894*, Cambridge, 1947, and particularly Hans Rogger, "America in the Russian Mind—or Russian Discoveries of America," *The Pacific Historical Review*, Vol. 47, No. 1 (February 1978), pp. 27–51.

18. Hans Rogger, "Amerikanizm and the Economic Development of Russia," *Comparative Studies in Society and History*, Vol. 23, No. 1 (January 1981), pp. 382–420.

SHARED DESTINY

A PARTICIPANT'S VIEW

George F. Kennan

The passage of the fifty-year interval since the establishment of Soviet-American diplomatic relations at the turn
of the year 1933–34 led to an intensive search by a large
number of people—publishers, editors, television inter-
viewers, arrangers of academic-lecture series, you name
them—for someone who was involved in that particular
episode and whose memories could instruct or divert
those today whose impressions of what it all amounted
to might be dim or nonexistent. There was a search, in
particular, for someone who could relate that event to
the previous state of Soviet-American relations and to the
immediately following years of the Stalin era. This search
soon revealed, to my surprise no less than to that of its
authors, that of all those thus directly involved in the
episode itself I appeared to be the sole survivor (on
either side), and of those who continued to serve in the
Soviet Union off and on through the remainder of the

Stalin period I alone seemed to have the dubious double distinction of being an eyewitness and trying to be a historian. The pressures, therefore, centered on me.

Others who have thought, studied, and written about as well as experienced much of a given phase of history will understand the distaste with which at an advanced stage of life one receives the suggestion that one should undertake an analytical effort to put the whole subject once again in historical perspective. Historical perceptions, like affairs de cœur, are a matter of a particular stage in one's life; attempts at repetition are unlikely to be successful. When my mind returns to the events in question, what comes to it is primarily the memories of individual experiences along the way. Some of them, it seems to me, speak for themselves; and I would rather recall them as they were, and let them tell their own story, than try to embroider them analytically.

With apologies to my own memoirs, in which most of the recollections had some sort of place, I offer a few of these recollections here to any who might like to know what it was like or (to borrow the common query of the TV interviewer) "how it felt" to be involved with Soviet-American relations at the moment of their establishment and in the ensuing years of Stalinist horror. To stress the responsibility of these memories in speaking for themselves and to distance the young man who received the experiences from the elderly one who now recalls them, I take the liberty of putting them in the narrative present.

I must begin at a point a bit more than fifty years ago—in 1932, to be exact—just before the establishment of diplomatic relations which we have lately been recalling. My wife and I are living, at this point, in Riga, Latvia. Latvia is a country that has until recently been part of the Russian Empire and will soon become part of the Soviet one but is now, for a twenty-year interval, independent. The atmosphere of the old, prerevolutionary

Russia still hangs over it. The city of Riga is itself a smaller edition of the prerevolutionary St. Petersburg, but without the palaces. The sleigh in which I am sometimes driven to the office in winter—a one-passenger open-air affair, in which the fur-coated passenger sits behind and below the massive figure of the bundled coachman on the box—is right out of Tolstoy. In summer, because we are poor, we live in a little wooden cottage out at the seashore. I commute on the suburban trains. The trains and the passengers, I among them, seem to be right out of Chekhov's stories. And if one goes farther into the countryside all that one sees—the cobbled roads, the swamps and fields, the birch trees and evergreen forests—are the purest Russia. I drink it all in, love it intensely, and feel myself for a time an inhabitant of that older Russia which I shall never see again in the flesh.

In the office, here in Riga, my work is the study of the Soviet Union. I have already been established as a Russian expert. I know the Russian language, and I, with two or three others, work, thoroughly and systematically, on the Soviet newspapers and magazines, reporting to our government on what they reveal of life in the Soviet Union. It is through these thousands of pages of small-type, poor-quality newsprint that I am obliged to form my first picture of the great Communist country that lies so near at hand and extends so far away to the east. I, like my colleagues, am appalled at the propaganda that pervades every page of this official Soviet literature—at the unabashed use of obvious falsehood, at the hypocrisy, and, above all, at the savage intolerance shown toward everything that is not Soviet. I am seized, as are my colleagues, with the desire to strip away this brazen façade, and to reveal, in my reports to Washington, the reality that lies beneath it. And I am surprised to find how easy it is, if one looks carefully and thoughtfully, to perceive what does lie beneath these gray and brittle pages, and to realize that the meaning of the propaganda is not in the literal text but in the subtle changes that occur in it from day to day—changes that every sophisticated Russian knows how to decipher and to interpret, as we ourselves, in time, learn to do. And this is my introduction to the Soviet Russia.

Let us jump ahead now to the days, just fifty years ago this past November, when diplomatic relations were being established between the United States and the Soviet Union. I happen at this time to be at home on leave of absence, and I am chosen to accompany, as interpreter and diplomatic secretary, our first Ambassador to the Soviet Union, Mr. William C. Bullitt, on his journey to Moscow, where he is to present his diplomatic credentials.

Bullitt is a striking man: young, handsome, urbane, full of charm and enthusiasm, a product of Philadelphia society and Yale but with considerable European residence, and with a flamboyance of personality that is right out of F. Scott Fitzgerald—a man of the world, well educated, fluent in French and German, confident in himself, confident of the President's support, confident that he will have no difficulty in cracking the nut of Communist suspicion and hostility which awaits him in Moscow. He is not a radical, but he is not afraid of radicals. He was once a friend of John Reed, and he was later married, for a time, to Reed's widow.

From Le Havre, where the ship lands, we travel by train, via Paris and Berlin, to Moscow. The train takes two nights and a day. With us on the train is Maxim Litvinov, the Soviet Commissar for Foreign Affairs. He, too, has just been in Washington, negotiating the establishment of relations, and he is now returning to Moscow.

On the second day of that long railway journey, on a bitterly cold afternoon, when the train has been rolling for hours over the frozen fields of western Poland, we stop for a time at the Polish town of Bialystok, and Litvinov gets out and paces gloomily up and down the station platform, coat collar up against the wind. Bullitt goes out and joins him, and Litvinov then tells Bullitt as Bullitt later reports to me that this place, Bialystok, is actually the place where he was born and brought up; and he observes how strange it is for him to find himself there again after all this time, and confesses to Bullitt that he never wanted to be Soviet Foreign Minister in the first place—that his real ambition had always been to be a librarian. And from this very human confession I begin to realize what I am never to be allowed to forget: that these Soviet Communists with whom we will now have to deal are flesh-and-blood people, like us—misguided, if you will, but no more guilty than are we of the circumstances into which we all were born—and that they, like us, are simply trying to make the best of it.

Well, then, a few immensely exciting days later, Bullitt and I are standing with three or four other people in the middle of the vast parquet floor of one of the great empty ballrooms in the Kremlin palace, and Bullitt is giving his little speech and presenting his credentials to the titular head of the Soviet state—old Daddy Kalinin, as we used to call him—who is the only man of peasant origin in the Soviet leadership, and looks the part, with his venerable gray beard. And a few moments later Kalinin is speaking kindly to me, and telling me with what excitement and enthusiasm he and his friends, when they were young radical students, had read the books about Siberia written by my uncle, the elder George Kennan. The book was, Kalinin says, to my astonishment, the bible of the early Bolsheviks.

Such was the Russia of that day—and this. It could whipsaw you at times between its great extremes: the cold and the hot, the cruel and the tender, the callous and the humane.

Another change of scene. It is now my first winter in Moscow—the winter of 1933–34. Bullitt has gone home to organize an Embassy staff and has left me there for

two or three months as our first regular diplomatic representative in Communist Moscow. The Stalinist terror
has not yet begun, though it is not far off. The political
atmosphere is still relatively relaxed.

My wife has joined me. We are the first American
diplomatic couple to appear in the Moscow diplomatic
corps. We are sometimes invited to parties: marvellous
Russian-American parties in shabby Moscow apartments,
where nobody cares whether the apartments are shabby
or not, or where you are to put your coats, or what there
is to eat and drink—parties that are full of good talk,
endless talk, in the Russian manner. And later in the
evening we all go out to the great Park of Culture and
Rest along the Moscow River and skate down the broad
ice-covered paths from rink to rink, under the frozen
Russian stars, to the strains of the Viennese "Skater's
Waltz" rendered by scratchy loudspeakers somewhere up
in the trees.

Let us jump another two or three years ahead. It is now
1937. I am still in Moscow. But times have changed. Difficulties have arisen. The terrible Stalinist purges have
begun. Bullitt, disappointed and embittered (because he
was too impatient and wanted everything at once), has
left Russia, never to return. His place has just been taken
by a new Ambassador, a shallow and politically ambitious
man, whom Franklin Roosevelt is said to have appointed
to this job in a gale of laughter, because the man's wife
had financed fifteen senatorial campaigns and he had to
be in some way taken care of. ("Send him to Russia"
was the idea. "That will serve him right.")

The new Ambassador knows nothing about Russia—
has no serious interest in it. His only real interest is in
the publicity he can get at home. We are ashamed for
him before our diplomatic colleagues, not because of his
personal qualities or imperfections (I have no idea what
those were) but because of his obvious unfitness for the

job. To us, the Foreign Service officers stationed there, his having been sent out there as our chief seems like a gesture of contempt on the President's part for us and our efforts—a revelation of how little the American political establishment knows or cares about the Foreign Service. And it brings home to me for the first time that however much a Foreign Service officer may learn about the government to which he is accredited, he learns at least as much (and it is sometimes a bitter lesson) about the government he represents.

But to get back to my story: The purges are now at their height. The new Ambassador is invited to attend the second of the three great public purge trials—the visible tip of the immense iceberg of terror and cruelty which is now crushing Soviet society. He takes me with him as his interpreter, and I, sitting next to him, whisper into his ear what I can of the proceedings. He understands nothing of what is really going on. He even thinks the accused are genuinely guilty of the preposterous charges to which they are confessing; and he sententiously pronounces this opinion, during the intermission, to the assembled American journalists. But I do know what is going on; and the sight of these ashen, doomed men, several of them only recently prominent figures of the regime but now less than twenty-four hours away from their executions—the sight of these men standing there mumbling their preposterous confessions in the vain hope of saving themselves, or perhaps the members of their families, from disaster, the sight of their twitching lips, their prison pallor, their evasive, downcast eyes—is never to leave my memory. Nor is the impression mitigated by the fact that they would happily have seen the same thing done to others. Revolution is indeed, as someone has said, a beast that devours its own children.

Let us now move again some years ahead—several years this time. Many things have happened in those intervening years. I have served in a number of other places: Washington, Prague, Lisbon, London, and, finally, Berlin. But I am now once more in Russia. It is wartime—the final months of the Second World War. Averell Harriman is the Ambassador in Moscow—and an excellent Ambassador he is. I am his No. 2. The Russians are now our allies, and the Soviet Union is now winning victories. The building we live and work in faces the Kremlin across a great sea of asphalt pavement; and night after night we hear the booming of the gun salutes in celebration of the victories and see the fireworks rising triumphantly from Red Square.

I look on the war with mixed feelings. I have recollections of nearly three wartime years spent in Germany, most of that time in the early period of the war, before our country entered the contest. I have no love for Hitler. I have never questioned the necessity of defeating him. But I also have no hatred for the German people.

One July Sunday, I stand among the curbside spectators on one of the great circular boulevards of Moscow and watch fifty thousand German prisoners forced to march through the city at double time, as a spectacle for the Moscow populace. I have told about the episode in my memoirs.

It is a hot day. The sun beats down. The men, obviously just removed from the freight cars in which they have been transported, are weak, tired, and thirsty. But they are hounded along. Those who fall are pulled aside to be picked up later. Mounted guards ride their horses into those who show signs of lagging behind. It is a cruel spectacle. I don't doubt that the German Nazis are doing worse than this to many innocent people, here and elsewhere. But I am sickened. These young men are presumably draftees, most of them nineteen or twenty years old. They are no more responsible for the accident of birth that brought them to this place than are the young Russians who fight against them. They, like the rest of us, didn't choose their parents, or the time or the country of their birth. The crowds of Russian spectators, mostly women, look on impassively at this spectacle, but insofar as I can divine their real reactions from their eyes and their expressions these people are not devoid of sympathy for the prisoners. Russians—especially these Russians—have experienced too much of suffering not to feel for it when they see it before them.

It occurs to me, standing there at the curb, that in a great war like this the populations are all victims alike. Their fate and their sufferings bear no relation, as a rule, to the propaganda slogans and pretensions and professions of the governments that drive them to this slaughter. There are times and instances, I have no doubt, when a people has no choice but to stand up and fight. But such cases are rare, and I come away with the conviction that one should beware of all the collective hysterias of modern nationalism—the artificially fanned hatreds, the chauvinistic self-idealization, the professions of noble principle. The tragedies of war are a thousand times as deep as these hysterias, and put them all to shame.

We come now to the year 1945 and the month of May. It is victory day—the day of the ending of the war in Europe. The city of Moscow goes wild with joy and relief. People pour out onto the streets by the million. This is their day. They cannot be controlled; nor does anyone seriously try to control them.

The Party leaders, true to their ingrained habits, do try to channel the street demonstrations to places where the cheers and wavings will appear to be tributes to the regime's own wise war leadership. It does no good. To everyone's consternation and amazement, even to ours, the only place in Moscow where the crowds choose to gather and to demonstrate is the great square before the American Embassy. They crowd up against our walls in thousands, waving and cheering—they cannot be induced to go anywhere else. After some hours of this, I, being in charge of the Embassy at that moment, feel it necessary to acknowledge in some way this great demonstration of good will; and I go out onto one of the pedestals of the high half columns on the front of the building and say a few simple words to the crowd in Russian, congratulating them on the common day of victory. They love it and roar their approval. But Stalin, learning of it, resents it intensely. It is the first time a bourgeois representative has been publicly cheered by a Soviet crowd. This is taken by Stalin as a humiliation, and I should know that someday I shall be made to pay for it if there is any way he can cause me to do so.

A few more months pass. It is the winter of 1946. The war has ended. The problems of policy are now those of the postwar future. In mid-February, Averell Harriman is away for a time, and again I am left in charge of the Embassy. I am ill in bed, as I recall it, with a severe sinus infection. Among the incoming telegrams brought to me one morning for my consideration is one from the Department of State informing me that the Russians are declining to join the World Bank and the International Monetary Fund. The Department professes bewilderment over the reasons for this attitude. Why, it asks me, should the Russians decline to take part? How do I explain it?

I am filled with impatience and disgust at this naïveté. For two years, I have been trying to persuade people in Washington that the Stalin regime is the same regime we knew in the prewar period, the same one that conducted the purges, the same one that concluded the Non-Aggression Pact with the Nazis—that its leaders are no friends of ours. I have tried to persuade Washington that dreams of a happy postwar collaboration with this regime are quite unreal, that our problem is deeper than that; that Stalin and his associates are now elated with their recent military and political successes and think they see favorable prospects for extending their political

influence over all of Europe through the devices of infil-
tration and subversion. Until they are weaned from these
rosy hopes, I argue, it is useless for us to suppose that
they will participate in idealistic schemes for worldwide
collaboration under our leadership—particularly in such
areas as economics and finance, where their ideological
commitments are wholly different from our own.

To explain all this, I sit down and draft a preposter-
ously long telegram—some eight thousand words, if I remember correctly—going right back to the beginning and
describing, as though in a primer for schoolchildren, the
nature, the ambitions, the calculations of these men. It is
a grim and uncompromising picture. I wonder uneasily
what the reaction will be at home. To my amazement, it
is instantaneous and enthusiastic. The telegram goes the
rounds in official Washington—to the other departments
and to the White House. It is even made required reading for hundreds of senior military officers. For the first
time in my life (and the last, incidentally), I seem to be
on the same wavelength as official Washington. But,
more important and more significant than that, I seem
to have aroused a strain of emotional and self-righteous
anti-Sovietism which in later years I will wish I had not
aroused.

The scene shifts to Washington in the years 1947–1949.
I have been given a high position with policymaking responsibilities in the Department of State. It is still primarily Soviet-American relations that I am concerned
with; but the problem now is with my own government,
not with the Soviet one. I have my own concept of what
American policy should be in this immediate postwar
period. It is a simple concept: first, of course, to pursue
"containment," in the sense of restoring economic health
and political self-confidence to the peoples of Western
Europe and Japan in order that they may be resistant to

local Communist pressures; and to prove to the men in the Kremlin, in this way, that they are not going to succeed in extending their rule to further areas by political intrigue and intimidation, that they cannot serve their own interests without dealing with us; and then, when a political balance has been created, to proceed to the negotiation with Moscow of a general political settlement.

Well, the first part of this concept proceeds without difficulty. The Marshall Plan, which is an integral part of it, is marvellously successful. And something very similar is accomplished, primarily on my initiative, for Japan. The time for negotiations, as I see it, is approaching. Here the difficulties begin. The subject of any real negotiations with the Russians would have to be the removal of the unfortunate division of Germany and Europe to which the final operations of the recent war have led. But our European allies do not want that, nor does the emerging German leader, Konrad Adenauer; and the Secretary of State agrees with them. They all mistake the Soviet threat for a military one, and feel that there must be a military response, in the form of the NATO alliance. I am not enthusiastic. I feel that this will cause us to take our eye off the ball of economic recovery. I particularly deplore the idea of bringing West Germany in as a partner. This, I maintain, will freeze the division of Europe and make it impossible to remove, and will create bitter problems for the future. But I am overruled. Military thinking, here and in Europe, has taken over from political thinking. People are reverting to nineteenth-century patterns of thought—and this in the nuclear age, to which, it seems to me, these patterns are not relevant. But I can do nothing to stop it. I also disagree with our government's intention of developing the hydrogen bomb. Robert Oppenheimer and I would both prefer to have another try at negotiation with the Russians before we take this fatal step. Again, I am overridden. So in mid–1950 I give up my job as head of the Planning Staff, am granted, at my request, a long leave of absence without pay (for at this point they are glad to get rid of me), and go off to Princeton to try to become a scholar.

But the respite is not long. Only a few months pass before I am called to Washington again and appointed Ambassador to Moscow. The assignment has nothing to do with Soviet-American relations. The present Ambassador, it seems, is leaving. It is the election year of 1952. For purely domestic-political reasons, the Administration is afraid to leave the post vacant. Foreign policy—policy toward the Soviet Union—plays no part in the decision. It never occurs to people in the Administration that the position of American Ambassador to Moscow has anything to do with policy toward the Soviet Union. They don't really know, to tell the truth, what an ambassador is for. But it suits their book that someone should be out there, at this politically delicate moment, to keep the chair warm. So now I am again in Moscow, but this time in the lofty and lonely position of Ambassador.

Gone now is the familiarity with one's Foreign Service colleagues which marked the earlier years in that city. I reside in the solitary splendor of Spaso House. But it is a gilded cage. The political atmosphere could not be worse. The Korean War is still on. People on both sides expect it soon to develop into a real Soviet-American war. The Embassy is isolated from the population as never before. I, as Ambassador, am the Soviet Union's Enemy No. 1. The walls of the Embassy compound are floodlit from the outside and patrolled by armed guards, like a prison. Five burly gentlemen—all carefully picked colonels of the internal and border guards—are stationed at the gate day and night. Wherever I go, whether on foot or by car, they accompany me. Never did anyone have more constant companions. We politely salute each time I come out; but we never speak. Yet as the months go by—the months of this constant silent companionship—I see that they are doing their duty faithfully, as I am trying to do mine. And I sense, growing up between us, a certain tacit, helpless sympathy; for, once again, what are we all if not the products of the accidents of birth?

On some of the warm summer nights, we walk—this odd little cortege—among the crowds in the Park of Culture and Rest, where once, in happier times, I skated. We are anonymous here. We merge with the crowds, for my guardians are in civilian clothes, and I am informally dressed and look much like anyone else. If the other people knew who I was, they would be interested but frightened, as would be my guardians; for it would be dangerous for anyone to have even the most casual conversation with me. So I walk among these crowds of people, observing them, hearing their conversation, near to them in one way but endlessly far from them in another; seeing but myself unseen; hearing but myself unheard. I console myself by fancying that I am an invisible disembodied spirit from another time or another planet, privileged to move about amid the life here below but never to participate in it, never to communicate with it, to be always near it but never part of it.

Next picture. It is still 1952, but a few more weeks have passed. I am now in Western Europe for a few days—in Geneva, where I have a young daughter in boarding school. I suddenly receive a phone call from the American Consulate General in that city. A telegram has been received from the Embassy in Moscow. The Embassy has just received a note from the Soviet Foreign Office saying that I am declared persona non grata, which means that they will no longer recognize me as Ambassador and I shall not be permitted to return to Moscow. The news has not yet been announced to the world press but will be shortly.

Within six months now of his own death Stalin is apparently in a strange state of anxiety and suspicion; and presumably he suspects me of God knows what.

I am thunderstruck. I cannot know, of course, that this will be the end of my Foreign Service career, but I know that it will mean a great change in my life. In one way or another, an epoch is ending for me. I also know that at any moment the world press will be tracking me down, demanding statements, interviews, photographs. I am not prepared for all this. It is too sudden. To give myself a little protection and a few moments to think about what has happened, I escape to a nearby movie house and sit there in the dark, trying to figure out what has happened to me and how I should respond to it. And shortly, to my intense disgust, I find myself watching with interest the silly movie, and I have to pinch myself to turn my eyes away from the screen and take account once again of my altered situation. In such absurdity, such human weakness, such childish helplessness, there comes to a rather ignominious end some twenty years of official service in the Soviet Union.

I return home, of course, with my family. The Presidential election of 1952 has just taken place. A new Administration—in some respects like the one we have today—has installed itself in the seats of power in Washington. No one having said anything to me about what I am now to do, I live quietly through the winter at our farm in the country. The weeks go by. Finally, I myself ask to come to Washington to see the new Secretary of State. He receives me civilly, and casually tells me that he knows of no niche for me in the Department or in the Foreign Service. I am, in other words, fired. No reason is offered. But, says he, before you go I would like you to give me your impressions of the situation in Russia today. I pull myself together and do this. "Well, well," he says. "You know, when you talk about these things you interest me. Very few people do. I hope you will come down here from time to time and let me have your views on what is happening in Russia."

I ask him how it is proposed to announce my dismissal to the press and the public. The Secretary says I should go to see his press secretary—he will work it out.

I go to see the press secretary. He professes helplessness. "Honestly, I wouldn't know what to say," he says. "Would you have any suggestions?" I tell him I would like to have a few moments to think about it. So I go out to a restaurant for lunch, take out a piece of paper, and draft, so to speak, my own death warrant—the terms of my dismissal from the Foreign Service. I take it back to the press secretary, who reads it and says to me, "Geez, Mr. Ambassador, that's elegant—I couldn't have written that."

With these expressive words, twenty-six years of foreign service, and twenty years of official involvement with Soviet-American relations, years always full of irony, come to an ironic end.

Well, thirty years have now gone by since I left the government service. I have continued to be involved with Russia, both czarist and Soviet, but this time as a historian —no longer as a participant. Some of the books I write deal with the final years of the prerevolutionary Russia and the first years of the Soviet one. The work is not unrewarding. I come to know my principal historical characters—the heroes or antiheroes of my books—as though I had known them in the flesh. I relive, together with them, their times, their struggles, their disappointments. I know, as they could not know, that they are all actors in what will ultimately be seen as a tragic drama; but I try to judge them for what they were, and for what they knew. And I find it striking that here, again, as in all the years of official service in Russia, I am myself remote from the people I am observing. I see them again, as I once saw the Soviet Union in Riga, through the record of the printed word; but I must myself remain unseen, as I was on the paths of the Park of Culture and Rest—

must always be near to what interests me but never be *of* it.

I would like, of course, to be able to communicate to those now in power something of what I see through these historical lenses; for I fancy myself to perceive, in these records of the past, lessons that, if they were closely looked at, could help us all to identify the hopeful roads into the future and to refrain from entering, and from pulling others along with us, on those paths at the end of which there is no hope, and from which no one ever returns. The efforts I make in this direction are not crowned, as a rule, by any conspicuous success; but that is not important. There are certain professions, such as medicine, teaching, and the priesthood, where one does not inquire anxiously into the results of one's efforts; and the writing of history is one of them. The effort, here, is its own reward. The results are the concern of a Higher Authority.

THE FIRST FIFTY YEARS

John Lewis Gaddis

It has been more than fifty years since an eager and excited William C. Bullitt, accompanied by a nervous, young, Russian-speaking assistant named George Kennan, arrived in Moscow to establish the first American embassy that had ever existed in that city. There had been no diplomatic relations with the Soviet Union since the October revolution in 1917 and no diplomatic establishment in that country since the American embassy had removed itself, first from Petrograd, then Vologda, early in the following year.[1] Expectations ran high that the resumption of official relations would bring substantial benefits to both countries: trade would mushroom, and there was the hope, on both sides, of common action to counter the growing power of Germany and Japan. It is a measure of how high these hopes were that President Roosevelt was willing to accept at face value Foreign Minister Maxim Litvinov's assurances that Moscow had no connection with, or interest in, the fortunes of the Communist Party of the United States and that religious freedom was and would be respected in the Soviet Union. Stalin followed suit with a grand promise to build the Americans an embassy on a bluff overlooking Moscow, modeled on Thomas Jefferson's Monticello.

It took less than a year for the hopes that both sides had entertained to be disappointed. Trade shrank. Cooperation against Germany and Japan proved to be impossible to work out. Communism in the United States continued to be suspended on cables from Moscow (thus giving rise to the old riddle: Why is the Communist Party of the U.S.A. like the Brooklyn Bridge?); religious freedom continued not to flourish inside the U.S.S.R. And, somehow, Monticello in Moscow never got built.[2]

One can see, then, in just this first year of Soviet-American diplomatic relations, the alternation between euphoria and distrust that has characterized them ever since. It is symbolic—and perhaps appropriate, given the history—that the formal joint commemoration of this fiftieth anniversary by the Soviet Academy of Sciences and the American Historical Association, scheduled to be held in Kiev in October 1983, had to be postponed until the following spring because relations were so bad.

We in the West, in trying to understand the ups and downs of our relations with the Russians, tend to take on some of that air of plaintive incomprehension demonstrated by Professor Henry Higgins in *My Fair Lady*: Why do the Russians behave the way they do? Why can't they be more like us?

History—the discipline I represent—provides no definitive answers to this question. It lacks, and always will lack, the explanatory precision of physics or chemistry; it recognizes that just because something has happened a certain way in the past is no guarantee for the future, whatever the political scientists may say. Nor do we historians communicate the provisional conclusions we do have as effectively as we might. When given a choice between being profound and being prolix, we will choose the latter every time. We resist the notion that we ought to make our findings useful to others—with the not very surprising result that we exchange them mostly among ourselves. Then we sit back, grimacing at each disaster that occurs, exchanging helpful comments like: "Too bad they don't listen to historians."

Nevertheless, it ought not to be impossible to distill, from our half-century of diplomatic contacts with the Soviet Union, a few succinct and reasonably comprehensible propositions that might be of use in thinking about these relations in the future. To be sure, any such effort should surround itself with all the caveats that ought to accompany attempts to draw "lessons" from the past— propositions of this nature are, of necessity, oversimplifications, subject to all of the qualifications and quibbles in which historians like to indulge. But if we are going to learn anything at all from history, then some generalization is unavoidable. Otherwise, to adopt former Secretary of State Haig's terminology, we risk "caveating" ourselves into complete uselessness and incomprehensibility.

In this spirit, then, the first proposition I put forward in attempting to account for our difficulties with the Soviet Union derives from one of the few fairly reliable "laws" of history: where great power is found in conjunction with great insecurity, some form of imperialism is likely to result.

By power I mean quite simply the capacity, chiefly through the use of military force, to assert one's will in world affairs. (This attribute is rather different from influence—the extent to which one succeeds in asserting one's will—a point I will come back to later.) Now, by this standard, the Soviet Union must certainly rank as one of the two most important nations in the world today, given its combined military and industrial strength. It obtained this power by a particular combination of geographical and historical circumstances: the sheer size and resources of Russia itself, which as Alexis de Tocqueville pointed out a century and a half ago,[3] would have guaranteed any government of that country, whatever its political orientation, considerable weight in world affairs; the European civil wars of the period 1914–1945, which resulted in the destruction of Germany, the only significant center of countervailing power on the Eurasian continent; and the ruthless and single-minded determination on the part of Soviet leaders, both before and after World War II, to accumulate economic and military strength as a matter of state policy.

Insecurity may seem inconsistent with the accumulation of power, but one of the most striking characteristics of the Soviet Union is that the great power it has obtained over the years has not given that country or its leaders anything approaching a sense of self-assurance. There are several reasons for this: the historic vulnerability of the Russian state, which has never enjoyed easily defensible borders and which tends, more than most other states, to see in the simple existence of concentrations of power beyond its control a threat to its own survival; the nature of the Soviet regime itself, which came into power by conspiratorial means and maintains itself in power by repression, at no point possessing the self-confidence necessary to submit itself to the legitimizing function of free elections; and the role of ideology, which provides in another form an excuse for the Soviet regime's existence, but only by picturing the outside world as both decadent and dangerous, as headed for the ash-heap of history on the one hand and having the capacity and the will, if not resisted, to crush the Soviet state on the other.

It is this combination of power and insecurity that produces what I call imperialism. I use this term not in the sense of seeking colonies, markets, and raw materials overseas, as it was used in the nineteenth century, or as an imprecation hurled at the policies of the non-Communist world, as the Russians use it today, but as the conviction on the part of one great nation that its security interests require the indefinite expansion of its influence at the expense of the security interests of others. Or, to put it another way, confusing one's vital interests with one's peripheral interests to such an extent that one does not know where to stop.[4]

From a historian's perspective, there is nothing uniquely Communist or capitalist in this tendency: imperial Germany had it in the late nineteenth and early twentieth centuries; indeed, that country's behavior provides a far more appropriate analogy to the current policies of the Soviet Union than does the more frequently applied comparison with Nazi Germany. Nor is this tendency anything new; after all, one of the very best books about the rise and fall of an imperial mentality is Thucydides's *The Peloponnesian Wars*, written some 2,400 years ago. Nor should we in this country be so short-sighted as to believe ourselves wholly exempt from this tendency, as the long and unhappy history of our involvement in Indochina attests.

But of the nations subject to imperial tendencies today, the Soviet Union, by any reasonably objective standard, stands out in that it so consistently seeks to project its influence with so little regard to the security interests of others. To a far greater degree than the United States and its allies, it is not content with the status quo in world affairs and sees its own security as requiring changes in it. It is worth stressing again that communism has relatively little to do with this Russian imperial drive. If by some magic Alexander Solzhenitsyn were put in charge of the Politburo tomorrow, the combination of power and insecurity would still be there and would still be likely to produce the same result.

We have to recognize that: the Russians do not share our view of the world and are not likely to; we will for

years to come find it easier to identify common interests
with nations as diverse as China, Saudi Arabia, Yugoslavia, and Finland than with the Soviet Union; and
questions of war or peace will hinge, in large part, on the
way in which we and the Russians manage the very great
differences we will continue to have.

Certain postulates regarding Soviet behavior flow from
this imperial framework of analysis and from the experiences of the past half-century. The first is that, in dealing
with a power that equates security with expansion, one
cannot expect to have unilateral restraint reciprocated. A
perennial criticism of American policy over the years has
been that we, rather than the Russians, have determined
the course of Cold War competition, that Russian behavior has been for the most part a response to escala-
tions on our part, and that greater restraint on our side
would have induced greater moderation on theirs.

If this were true, our problems would be simpler. But
the historical record is not very encouraging. During
World War II the United States hoped that its own
caution in asserting postwar political claims would induce
comparable moderation on the part of the Soviet Union
in Eastern Europe and elsewhere. This did not happen.
Recent research makes it clear that the Russians had begun work on a hydrogen bomb even before we decided
to build our own, after much worry over the possibility
of setting off a thermonuclear arms race.[5] A mutual withdrawal of Soviet and American occupation forces from
Korea took place in 1948–1949, only to have the Russians
then authorize their North Korean proxies to invade
South Korea. The Soviet Union began to develop long-
range strategic missiles before the United States did and
was the first overtly to threaten their use.[6] The Russians
sought to capitalize on the American decision not to invade Cuba following the Bay of Pigs fiasco in 1961 by
placing similar missiles on that island the following year.

Moscow did not reciprocate Washington's restraint in its strategic-missile programs in the mid-1960s, but continued its own rapid buildup of ICBMs and moved into the field of ABM technology as well. The Russians took advantage of a post-Vietnam reluctance to involve the United States in Third World conflicts and pushed their own interests in Africa, the Near East, Southeast Asia, and, most conspicuously, Afghanistan. However short the Europeans' memories on this point may be, it was the Soviet Union that upset the current nuclear balance on that continent through its deployment of the SS–20s in the mid–1970s. And, in 1983, the Russians shot down a South Korean airliner that had inadvertently strayed over sensitive military installations, despite repeated and apparently deliberate violations of comparably restricted United States airspace by Soviet and Cuban airliners that elicited nothing but reprimands.

I would not want this analysis to seem one-sided. There have been areas where the United States took the initiative in escalating the Cold War. One need only mention the Marshall Plan, NATO, the rearmament of West Germany, the Kennedy administration's post-missile-gap strategic buildup, the decision to deploy MIRVs, the human rights campaign of the late 1970s, and the Reagan administration's "evil-empire" rhetoric. But the United States, much more consistently than the Russians, has based its policies on the assumption that if we showed restraint, they would too. The historical record suggests that we ought not to count on that.

The second postulate the experience of the past half-century seems to confirm is that, as George Kennan pointed out in the famous "X" article in 1947,[7] the Russians are inclined to show restraint only when confronted with the fact or the prospect of countervailing power. They have been extremely careful—Afghanistan notwithstanding—in the way they have used their military forces over the years. They have demonstrated great caution in not allowing crises to escalate to the point that might risk war. In this sense, we are fortunate in our adversaries; they are not—like the adversaries we had in World War II—determined to achieve their objectives by any and all means.

This pattern of restraint in the face of actual or probable resistance has manifested itself in a variety of situations. The toleration Moscow has extended to Finland since the conclusion of the Russo-Finnish War in 1940 is probably a tribute to the fighting qualities the Finns displayed in that conflict, and presumably would again, should the occasion arise. It is significant how cautiously Stalin advanced his military and political claims in the Near East after World War II, yielding to American pressure on Iran and Turkey and, if Yugoslav accounts can be believed, to the prospect of a British as well as an American response on Greece.[8] The Soviet Union's failure to interfere with the Berlin airlift in 1948 demonstrated a clear respect for American military power and a determination not to let escalation proceed to the point where it might provoke war. Once the Russians became convinced that the Americans and their allies were not going to be pushed out of Korea, they authorized talks looking toward a cease-fire there.

Khrushchev's handling of the Berlin crises of 1958 and 1961 again showed restraint once it had become apparent, in each case, that the United States and its allies were going to stand firm. The Cuban missile crisis, at one level the supreme example of Soviet recklessness and irresponsibility, can at another level be seen as yet another manifestation of Soviet caution and restraint once the prospect of a tough Western response had become clear. Brezhnev grudgingly tolerated the American mining of Haiphong harbor virtually on the eve of the 1972 Moscow summit and backed off his threat to intervene in the Egyptian-Israeli war the following year after Nixon called the famous Defcon 3 military alert. And, finally, it should be noted that since 1981—compared to their behavior during the late 1970s—the Russians have shown remarkable caution in their dealings with the outside world, not least in their handling of the delicate Polish situation, and that this may have had something to do with an assessment on their part that the Reagan administration was determined to rebuild American military strength and not inclined to pussyfoot.

All of which only goes to show that the Russians are traditional practitioners of power politics: like most great nations in the past, they tend to exploit opportunities provided by the absence of countervailing power and to demonstrate caution and restraint where it is present. Once again, there is nothing at all Marxist about this; rather it is a pattern of behavior that should be familiar to any reasonably competent student of the history of international relations over the past several centuries. But it is historical perspective that is too often missing from our public and official speculations about Soviet behavior.

Containment, however, is not the whole story of our relationship with the Soviet Union over the years. Negotiations have, at times, proven to be a useful means of resolving tensions between our two countries; at other times they have been fruitless. Two very simple criteria have, I think, distinguished successful from unsuccessful negotiations; first, the extent to which the agreement sought reflected the interests of the two sides; and second, the extent to which compliance with its provisions could be monitored.

Examples of agreements that met those criteria include the Korean armistice of 1953, which though negotiated directly with the North Koreans and the Chinese Communists can be assumed to have been cleared with Moscow; the Austrian state treaty of 1955, which provided for the withdrawal of Allied and Soviet occupation forces and the establishment of Austria as an independent but neutral state; the Kennedy-Khrushchev "understanding" on Cuba, reached in the wake of the 1962 missile crisis and providing that the Russians would not station strategic weapons on the island in return for an American pledge not to invade it; the Limited Test Ban Treaty of 1963, prohibiting the testing of nuclear weapons in the atmosphere; the SALT I agreement of 1972, placing limits on numbers of ICBM launchers on both sides and banning anything other than the token deployment of ABMs; and the SALT II treaty of 1979, which although not ratified by the United States is considered to be sufficiently in the interests of both sides that both continue to observe it. What all these agreements had in common was the fact that, first, both we and the Russians had reasons to want them to work, and, second, means existed for each side to verify the other's compliance.

Conversely, agreements that have not met those criteria have tended not to hold up. Examples include the Roosevelt-Litvinov agreements of 1933, with their vague promises that the Russians would refrain from promoting revolutionary activities in this country, would respect religious freedoms within their own borders, and would arrange a settlement of prerevolutionary debts—all obligations easily undertaken in order to secure diplomatic recognition, but which Stalin probably had no intention of honoring; the 1945 Yalta agreements regarding the holding of free elections in Eastern Europe, which quickly became a sham, again because Stalin had no interest in having those elections take place and because the West had no means of ensuring that they did; the so-called agreement on "Basic Principles" to govern Soviet-American relations, signed at Moscow by Nixon and Brezhnev in 1972 and committing each nation to forgo attempts to achieve unilateral advantage at the expense of the other—this failed, again, because the Russians had no intention of giving up support for Third World "national liberation" movements and because there was no way for Washington to monitor Moscow's compliance; and the

1975 Helsinki agreements regarding human rights, where once again Moscow went along with something it did not intend to do in order to get something else—specifically, Western endorsement of post–World War II boundary lines in Eastern Europe. But it quickly became apparent that, in the absence of a sincere commitment to human rights on the part of the Russians, there was little the West could do other than document Soviet violations of these solemn and excessively optimistic agreements.

The point is that agreements between great nations are no better than the interests that lie behind them; no government is going to allow vital interests to be circumscribed by ink. Where those interests conflict, no number of carefully worded and lofty-sounding agreements is going to resolve the issue. But where interests are congruent —and despite the intensity and persistence of the Soviet-American rivalry, there are such areas of congruent interest—diplomacy can be useful, provided means exist to verify compliance.

There is another point to be kept in mind here. The agreements that failed had in common efforts in some way to change the behavior of the Soviet state. Whether the goal was to encourage religious freedom, to bring about free elections, to induce Soviet restraint in the Third World, or to promote human rights, the initiatives proceeded from the assumption that diplomacy could be used to bring about fundamental changes in the way great nations conduct their internal affairs. Negotiations, it was assumed, could provide not only a means of managing conflicts, but could also serve as instruments of reform.

Again, history offers little encouragement that this strategy works. Changes do occur within the Soviet Union. Indeed the changes we have witnessed since Stalin's time, at least insofar as the lot of the average Soviet citizen is concerned, are profound and, on balance, encouraging. But, as is the case in our system, these changes proceed chiefly from internal causes and are not susceptible to management or manipulation from the outside. To insist that diplomacy serve the interests of reform as well as those of global stability is to impose on it a task considerably beyond its capabilities. It is quite enough, for the moment, to concentrate on keeping the peace.

Another generalization that seems to be confirmed by our experience of dealing with the Russians over the years is that, whatever the course of diplomatic negotiations, the balance of power in the world—and the balance of terror, for that matter—has proven to be surprisingly stable. Without setting out in any conscious way, to do it, we have managed to create since World War II an international system that appears to tolerate considerable provocation without producing escalation among the great powers, and that, when it does produce escalation, seems capable of limiting it without recourse to major wars.

After all, we have had now four decades of competition with the Russians at the superpower level. No one would argue that this has been a gentlemanly contest; it has been full of dirty tricks, sneaky maneuvers, and belligerent posturing. It has witnessed the most enormous accumulation of military hardware the world has ever seen. And yet it has produced neither war nor the capitulation of either of the major antagonists. This, from a historian's point of view, is remarkable; one would be hard pressed to find in modern history comparable instances of great power rivalries that went on for so long, but with so little change in the respective positions of the major participants.

The main reason for this, it seems to me, is the stabilizing effect of the possession, on both sides and in vast quantities, of nuclear weapons.[9] One hears much these days about the destabilizing effects of such weapons, and undoubtedly these exist to a certain degree—the question of theater nuclear forces in Europe is an obvious example.

But overall the coming of the nuclear era has been beneficial in one very important respect: it has imposed a lid
on the process of escalation that was not present prior to
1945, and as a consequence provocations that almost certainly would in the past have led to a major war—the
Berlin blockade, the North Korean attack on South
Korea, the Quemoy-Matsu stalemate, the Berlin con-
frontations of 1958 and 1961, the Cuban missile crisis,
Vietnam, a whole series of Middle East flareups, and
Afghanistan—have not done so. Nor have these crises
produced dramatic changes in the overall power balance.
We have achieved a degree of stability that would have
been the envy of statesmen of the pre–World War I or
pre–World War II epochs, and we have very largely done
it without recognizing it.

All of this suggests that we ought not to get as excited
as we do about domino theories suggesting that if we
"lose" Vietnam, Iran, El Salvador, or Grenada the entire
foundation of our power in the world will erode. We
have had our setbacks, but so have the Russians. We did
lose Vietnam, but they lost China, which should be an
acceptable trade-off any day. We lost Ethiopia, but they
lost Egypt. We lost Iran, but they certainly have not
gained it. We lost Cuba and may have lost Nicaragua,
but what the Russians have acquired is highly question-
able, given the costs involved. Afghanistan makes the
point even more clearly. International relations, in short,
are not tennis matches, and it is misleading to look at
them in that way.

Nor is the "balance of terror," as Churchill described
the arms race, as delicate as some would have us believe.
History offers little reason to expect one side, through
some sudden technological breakthrough, to gain a decisive edge over the other. After all, any decision to
launch a disarming first strike would require assuring
one's self with 100 percent certainty that nothing that
could go wrong would; and if experience is any guide at
all, this would be an extremely shaky assumption. Who-

ever Murphy was, his is one of the most reliable laws we have, and fortunately it works in Russia as well as here. The lesson seems to be that we can tolerate certain asymmetries in the arms race—at least up to a point—and that so-called window-of-vulnerability arguments ought to be treated with a healthy amount of skepticism.

This is by no means to say that the risks of nuclear war are not and should not be matters of great concern, for yet another fairly reliable lesson of history is that where weapons exist excuses are found to use them. Nor is it at all clear that deterrence would not work as well with half, or even a quarter, of the weapons available to both sides. But the point is that deterrence has worked now for quite a long time, that nuclear weapons have provided the means to make it work, and that those who advocate their abolition—or their unilateral reduction—are under some obligation to indicate what might replace them in performing this very valuable function.

The final proposition I put forward, based on what we know of the evolution of Soviet-American competition, is that power is not the same as influence; that there is no precise correlation between the amount of influence great states command and the military power they can bring to bear.

Any reasonably objective assessment of the military balance would conclude, I think, that today the power of the Soviet Union relative to that of the United States is greater than it was, say, at the beginning of the Nixon administration a decade and a half ago. The Russians have long since surpassed us in numbers of strategic missiles, have maintained their long-standing conventional-force superiority in Europe, and have mounted for the first time a significant challenge to the U.S. Navy's position on the high seas.

But can one conclude from this that the Russians have more influence in the world than they had in 1969?

Again, an objective assessment would have to answer no. In 1969 the United States was bogged down in a costly and unpopular war in Indochina; the "opening" to China had not yet taken place; the Russians enjoyed considerable prestige and influence in the Middle East where few people had yet heard of Anwar Sadat; the economies of the Soviet Union and its East European satellites had not yet begun the obvious decline that has since made them so unattractive as models for the rest of the world; and despite events in Czechoslovakia the year before, the Soviet record on human rights had not gained the notoriety it now possesses.

Today military power appears to be the only way left to the Soviet Union to gain influence in the world, and as we have had occasion to learn, the process of translating one into the other is by no means automatic. Our own influence, if anything, has grown in the past decade, partly as a result of our extrication—however painful—from Vietnam, partly as a result of the still-not-sufficiently appreciated diplomatic skills of Henry Kissinger in the early 1970s, but mostly because of the Russians' manifest ineptitude, inefficiency, and brutality. It is ironic that a nation should lose influence as it accumulates power, but that is precisely the situation that confronts Soviet leaders today.

And that is the only circumstance that might disrupt the global geopolitical equilibrium that has been so striking a feature of the postwar era; for the Russians, despite their power, are likely to feel more and more isolated as time goes on. That situation—the development on their part of a bunker mentality—presents real dangers from our point of view. It may not be beyond the realm of possibility that we might at some point consider it to be in our interest to try to preserve rather than to undo a certain amount of Soviet influence in the world, both because of our own stake in maintaining an overall balance of power and because of our fear of what might happen if the Soviet Union should come to see itself—as it may in fact do in the not-too-distant future—as an empire in danger of imminent collapse.

What conclusions, then, might we draw from our experience of dealing with the Russians during the past half-century? What might we do to ensure that the next fifty years, providing we all manage to get through them, are not as acrimonious as the past fifty have been? Because the relationship is bilateral, there is a limit to what American policy alone can accomplish. It takes two to tango, and the Russians have more than once demonstrated an unwillingness to take the floor when we were ready to do so, as we from time to time have rejected their invitations. Still, there are four attitudes we might develop to cultivate a more cooperative attitude on Moscow's part: firmness, flexibility, consistency, and civility. Let me try to demonstrate that these are not as contradictory as they seem.

Firmness. Harry Truman used to say, drawing on his extensive experience in Missouri politics, that the only way to get the attention of a mule was to hit him over the head with a two-by-four. There is reason to believe that he found this maxim applicable to foreign affairs, and especially to the problem of dealing with the Russians. Truman was not always as restrained in his pronouncements as one might like—certainly this was a source of unending regret to Mrs. Truman. A translation of his two-by-four proposition into the polite language of diplomacy might be this: Firmness is a way of opening the path to dialogue, a notion that we might keep in mind for the future.

For we have, in our policies toward the Russians over the years, alternated between attempts to win their trust through policies of restraint and openhandedness and efforts to get their attention by keeping the military equivalent of a two-by-four within close reach. And the sad fact is that we have, on the whole, done better with the second approach than with the first. The Russians understand and respect power, but they tend to confuse restraint on our part with the creation of tempting opportunities for them. The first step toward a permanent improvement in Soviet-American relations, therefore, appears to be a clear and unwavering determination on our part to keep up our end of the balance of power.

Flexibility. We need to keep in mind as well, though, that containment is only a means to an end, not an end in itself. When firmness produces opportunities to compromise or resolve differences on a basis acceptable to both sides, then one must have the flexibility to explore and, if feasible, to accept them. Such opportunities have presented themselves in the past, as the history of our negotiations with the Soviet Union has shown. Provided we apply to these negotiations the criteria of mutual interest and mutual verifiability, there is no reason we should not pursue them in the future, even at the risk of occasionally alarming our allies.

For alliances, like containment, are means to the greater end of ultimately reducing tensions; they are not ends in themselves. And yet, more opportunities to negotiate reductions of tension with the Russians have been lost for fear of unraveling our alliances than from any other single cause.

Consistency. To obtain the necessary balance between firmness and flexibility, we need more centralized authority over our foreign policy than we have been able to maintain during the past decade. The Russians have a point, after all, when they complain that they never know who they should be negotiating with on the American side—the State Department, the National Security Council, the Pentagon, the Congress, the Chamber of Commerce, the AFL-CIO, or some presidential candidate. We need to "get our act together" better than we have done recently, and that means going back to the startling idea of actually having somebody—anybody, one might almost add—in charge of foreign policy.

We might also think about how better to insulate foreign and national-security policy from the whims and caprices of domestic politics. It is in the nature of national-security policy that it concerns itself with issues of long-term national interest, while domestic politics deals with the transitory and often opportunistic concerns of party, faction, and even individuals. And yet, we regularly and with increasing frequency subordinate the requirements of the first to the demands of the second. Aspirants for the presidency define their positions not on the basis of where the national interest lies, but in terms of what their pollsters tell them the public wants to hear. Those who succeed then face the problem of matching campaign commitments to the very different circumstances of the real world. This process of accommodating rhetoric to reality takes longer with each new administration; the consequence is to produce the volatility, instability, and indeed most of the ineffectiveness for which American foreign policy has become noted over recent years. It is difficult to believe that the Constitution demands—or that public opinion requires—such a haphazard way of conducting world affairs.

Civility. As Mr. Nixon—not always one to follow his own good advice—used to say, we need to lower our voices. It would be difficult to overestimate the damage our leaders' incautious rhetoric has done to our relations with the Russians during the past decade. Jimmy Carter and Ronald Reagan may have had little in common, but they did manage to convince the Soviet leadership of their determination to undermine it—Carter through his human rights campaign, Reagan through his characterization of the U.S.S.R. as the "focus of evil in the modern world." [10] They did this, not out of any actual desire to challenge the Kremlin's authority, but as a cheap and easy way to gratify certain domestic constituencies. As it turned out, though, the diplomatic consequences remained long after the domestic occasions that had given rise to these pronouncements had been forgotten. There is an obvious value in maintaining a clear distinction between policies that challenge a state's expansionism for the purpose of maintaining a balance of power and policies that call into question a state's legitimacy for the purpose of undermining it. Yet that distinction recently has not come across as clearly as it might have in our dealings with Moscow.

There is a particular irony in the fact that the Russians should be so sensitive about this, because no nation has blurred that distinction in its own behavior more than the Soviet Union. Moscow's rhetorical assaults on the United States and its allies regularly continue to surpass, in stridency, vituperation, and sheer outrageousness, even the most extreme pronouncements of Reagan or any other Western statesman.[11] The difference is that we expect such statements from Moscow and do not take them seriously. The Russians, when we make them, do.

What we always ought to keep in mind in dealing with the Russians is that, next to security, they want respect most: they still see themselves as newcomers in the great-power club, and like all newcomers they are exceedingly sensitive to the slights and insults they may receive from others, even as they engage in them vigorously themselves. If the Americans have a Henry Higgins mentality in looking at the Russians, then it seems fair to say that the Russians have a Rodney Dangerfield attitude toward the United States. They feel they just don't get the respect to which their status in world affairs entitles them. It would not cost us a great deal to grant them that.

Few, if any, of us will be present a half-century from now to commemorate the one hundredth anniversary of Soviet-American diplomatic relations. But let us hope that our absence from that occasion will result from the gradual and inexorable ravages of old age, rather than from more abrupt and cataclysmic ravages we can all imagine, however fortunate we have been, thus far, in actually avoiding them.

I make no claim that the study of history offers us any reliable way of getting to that point. After all, the professional posture of constantly facing backward is not well calculated to induce confidence in one's ability to see the next bend in the road, much less the ultimate destination. For precisely this reason, I have some qualms about actually putting a historian in the driver's seat. Certainly the few instances in which that has been done do not reinforce one's assurance that this would be a wise way to proceed. At the same time, though, few forward-looking drivers would want to get out on the road without some kind of rear-view mirror, not only to give an idea of how far they have come, but also of who, or what, is about to overtake them.

Perhaps it is in this way that history can be of some value in getting us, or our descendants, to that anniversary celebration in 2033. It gives us no sure guidance for the future. It certainly will not anticipate every surprise that may lie along the way. But, like a rear-view mirror, history can serve, in the onrushing course of events, as a small reminder of how comparable crises have been surmounted in the past, of what has worked and what has not, of where contemporary problems fit within the larger context. And that, we historians like to think, has its uses.

NOTES

1. George F. Kennan's *Russia Leaves the War* (Princeton, 1956) still provides the best account of the break in relations that followed the Bolshevik Revolution.
2. Thomas R. Maddux, *Years of Estrangement: American Relations With the Soviet Union, 1933–1941* (Tallahassee, 1980), pp. 11–43.
3. Alexis de Tocqueville, *Democracy in America,* J. P. Mayer and Max Lerner, eds., trans. George Lawrence (New York, 1969), pp. 378–379.

4. For a definition of *imperialism* that takes into account the generalized concern of great powers to maintain global influence, see Tony Smith, *The Pattern of Imperialism* (Cambridge, 1981), pp. 6–7.
5. David Holloway, *The Soviet Union and the Arms Race* (New Haven, 1983), pp. 23–25.
6. See Arnold L. Horelick and Myron Rush, *Strategic Power and Soviet Foreign Policy* (Chicago, 1966).
7. "X" [George F. Kennan], "The Sources of Soviet Conduct," *Foreign Affairs*, Vol. XXV (July 1947), pp. 566–582.
8. Milovan Djilas, *Conversations with Stalin*, trans. Michael B. Petrovich (New York, 1962), p. 182.
9. One may advance this notion regarding superpower behavior, I trust, without being placed in the position of agreeing with Kenneth Waltz's recent suggestion that continued nuclear proliferation might have the same effect. See his article, "Toward Nuclear Peace," in Robert J. Art and Kenneth N. Waltz, eds., *The Use of Force*, 2d ed. (Lanham, Maryland, 1983), pp. 573–601.
10. Reagan speech to the National Association of Evangelicals, Orlando, Florida, March 8, 1983, *Weekly Compilation of Presidential Documents*, 19 (March 14, 1983), pp. 367–369.
11. See "Russia's anti-Reagan Campaign," *Economist*, 291 (June 23, 1984), p. 34.

THE HIGH COST
OF ILLUSIONS

Adam B. Ulam

Much of the discussion of Soviet-American relations in the West could be summarized by the titles of two celebrated, if for the contemporary public unreadable, nineteen-century Russian novels: *Whose Fault Is It?* and *What Is To Be Done?* Has the parlous course of relations between the two countries, at times dangerously close to an actual confrontation, resulted from a Soviet quest for world domination or a Soviet desire to strike at the vital interests of the democratic world? Or has the fault lain with the United States, whose policy-makers through sins of omission and commission have aggravated if not provoked those conflicts and tensions that have characterized the unhappy coexistence of the two powers since World War II? I do not have to expatiate on the various themes propounded by the partisans of the opposing views. The very existence of the Soviet system and its leaders' ambitions are for some incompatible with a peaceful international order; no, reply those on the other end of the spectrum, it is Washington that through its championship of the cause of reaction and through its defense of an unjust status quo all over the world has aroused the Soviets' suspicions and hostility and compelled them to make countervailing moves.

Less ideological but acutely relevant to the current situation is the dispute betwen those who consider the recent prodigious Soviet buildup in nuclear and conventional arms as clear proof that the Kremlin is bent on expansion through intimidation, if not indeed war, and those, including some eminent American public figures, who see the Soviet military posture as defensive and who place much, if not most, of the blame for the arms race on the American military-industrial complex and on those conservative forces on the American political scene for whom the very idea of negotiating with the Russians is distasteful.

The debate about the responsibility for the present unhappy state of affairs influences the various prescriptions for its resolution or amelioration. If the U.S.S.R. resembles the picture painted by its vilifiers, then the only logical stance for the United States, until and unless the Soviet system changes, is one of armed vigilance and instant reaction to any attempt by Moscow to expand its sphere of influence. If this picture is false, then the U.S. should reexamine its own policies and enter a real and far-reaching dialogue with the U.S.S.R., rather than trying to conjure away its real or imaginary fears through more weapons, counterinsurgency, economic sanctions, and all those other policies that have been tried and found largely wanting during the last forty years.

II

The argument between these points of view, though not without historical or philosophical interest, is to my mind of little practical help in resolving the main problems of

Soviet-American coexistence or even in understanding them. We must first of all strive to understand the inherent difficulties in the relations between two countries. On what might be called the mechanical side of the dilemma, there is the vexing problem of communication. Since the end of World War II, there have been a number of treaties and agreements between the United States and the U.S.S.R., summit meetings between their leaders, and a continuous flow of diplomatic notes and contacts. But has all that intercourse resulted in either side's having a clear understanding of the other's real goals, fears, and motivation for agreement (or disagreement)? No. Witness the ephemeral nature of those "spirits" of Geneva, Camp David, etc., and the almost immediate disillusionment (at least on the American side) about détente following what at first seemed a very important and reassuring series of agreements before and during the Nixon-Brezhnev summit of 1972.

It is therefore understandable that some American statesmen and observers have concluded that it is hopeless to negotiate with the Russians, or that the U.S. can negotiate only from a position of superior strength to avoid finding itself with the short end of the bargain. How can such a democracy as ours, with its policy options openly discussed in the Congress and the media, subject to pressures and criticisms both by its citizens and its allies, deal on equal terms with the representatives of a system where not only the ultimate decisions, but the very process by which they are arrived at, are confined to some twenty men—members of the Politburo—and where even the highest government and military officials, unless members of that body, are seldom privy to the reasons behind any debate or division of opinion that might have preceded the formulation of the official Soviet stance?

If pressed on the point and given a truth serum, a Soviet spokesman would admit that much of the above is true. But then he might reciprocate by pointing out the problems that Soviets face when dealing with the Americans, the difficulty they encounter in seeking meaningful agreements with a country where the most important political issues are often affected by volatile and unpredictable moods of public opinion. And even when briefed by Georgii Arbatov* or some comparably knowledgeable Americanologist, the average Politburo member must find it hard to understand the illogic that colors American thinking on foreign affairs.

The Americans, our Politburo member might recall, who accepted it as a fact of life when Eastern Europe lay supine under Stalin's iron heel, reacted with outbursts of indignation in 1956 and 1968 when, after granting Hungary and Czechoslovakia a degree of autonomy unimaginable in Stalin's day, the Kremlin felt constrained to intervene to prevent these countries from lapsing into what it regarded as utter chaos that threatened the security of the entire Communist camp. While the United States was at the height of its power and had a crushing superiority in nuclear weapons, no American congressman would have dared to try to dictate to the Soviet government how it should treat its own citizens in such a public and peremptory fashion. But now that the U.S.S.R. is at least America's equal, the latter's politicians show no inhibitions about poking their noses into Soviet internal affairs. Our government, the Soviets would claim, has already exhibited great generosity in allowing a quarter-million disloyal citizens to emigrate, rather than throwing them into camps. Why should we comply with your preposterous demands informing us how many Jews should be allowed to leave or how we should deal with dissident X or Y? Would it not encourage you to make even more preposterous demands about issues that are none of your business?

Or, continues our Russian, take the strategic-arms

* Arbatov is the director of the Institute for the Study of the U.S.A. and Canada.

issue. Washington now loudly bewails Soviet superiority in ICBMs and has tried to persuade us to eliminate or reduce the number of heavy missiles, such as the SS-18. But wasn't it America's own leaders and military planners who decided in the 1960s that they did not need to match the U.S.S.R. in the number of long-range land-based rockets, or develop their own "heavy" missile? Some of your people talk hysterically about a "window of vulnerability" opening in the late 1980s and raise the danger of a Soviet preemptive strike. But we in Russia face a real and not imaginary danger as we look a decade or two ahead. Once industrialized, China is bound to possess—in addition to its almost limitless military manpower—a sizeable stock of nuclear weapons. And whatever the state of relations between Moscow and Beijing, we know that we can never trust the Chinese. Haven't they, even when weak and dependent on us, advanced brazen claims to Mongolia and more than hinted at similar claims on vast Asian areas of our country?

This recital of grievances and complaints on both sides could be considerably expanded. But instead let us examine a serious dispute in which a better American understanding of what lay beneath the surface of Soviet policies would have prevented real dangers. Not unexpectedly, such occasions may also illustrate the other side of the coin: Soviet misperceptions of American attitudes and motivations.

III

Next to the Korean war, the sharpest encounter during the Cold War occurred in 1948–1949, when the U.S.S.R. cut off land communications between the West and West Berlin. Thus, for most students of international affairs, the term "second Berlin crisis" is readily recognizable. It refers to those tension-filled years between November 1958 and October 1962, years that witnessed Khrushchev's ultimatums and other forms of threats and pressure, the ostensible purpose of which was to abrogate Western rights in Berlin and, some would add, to turn West Berlin into a constituent part of the German Democratic Republic.[1] To be sure, on the surface the Soviets appeared to be demanding merely that the United States and its allies agree to a German peace treaty that would acknowledge East Germany as a sovereign state that could control access to the Western enclave within its territory. If the West agreed, the U.S.S.R. intimated that it would be quite willing to persuade its German Communist friends to allow West Berlin to become a free demilitarized city. But if not, then Moscow declared that it would make its own peace treaty with the German Democratic Republic. As a sovereign power, the GDR would, Khrushchev more than hinted, institute a full blockade of the Western enclave. Were such a blockade to be challenged by NATO, the U.S.S.R. would not stand idly by and tolerate military moves or pressure directed against a fraternal socialist state. "Get out of West Berlin or war" was the prevailing Western interpretation of the Soviet stance. At times war seemed indeed very close. "I feel more gloomy about international developments than I have felt since the summer of 1939," wrote Arthur Schlesinger in August 1961, expressing the mood of President Kennedy's entourage in the wake of such recent developments as Khrushchev's attempt to bully the president in Vienna, the erection of the Berlin Wall, and the resumption of Soviet nuclear tests.[2]

Was West Berlin the real reason for the Soviets' menacing behavior during the four-year crisis? A careful study of Soviet moves before and during those critical years should, at least, suggest that the purpose of the Kremlin's threats, cajoleries, etc., might be quite different from the desire to add two million or so new subjects to its empire.

The prelude to the crisis must be found in the communiqué of the North Atlantic Council of December 1, 1957, stating that "NATO has decided to establish stocks of nuclear warheads ... intermediate range ballistic missiles will have to be put at the disposal of the Supreme Allied Commander in Europe." [3] In fact, the roots of the crisis and of the Soviet apprehensions that led to it bear some resemblance to certain features of the current East-West clash about the Euromissiles. Then, as now, the Atlantic Alliance proposed to deploy, one assumes mainly in West Germany, nuclear weapons capable of reaching targets within the U.S.S.R. Then, as now, missiles on West German soil constituted a special danger to the suspicious mind of the Kremlin. Never mind the formal provisions about NATO and its American commander's control of the deadly weapons. Sooner or later, by hook or by crook, the Soviets feared, Bonn would acquire its own nuclear armory.

To counter this possibility, the Kremlin at first tried a complicated diplomatic ploy, the Rapacki Plan, which though officially put forward by the Polish foreign minister in October 1957, was undoubtedly authored, down to the last comma, in Moscow. The plan proposed a nuclear-free zone in Central Europe composed of four countries: Poland, Czechoslovakia, and both Germanys. Under the plan, no atomic, hydrogen, or rocket weapon would be produced or deployed within the zone. Thus, as on many other occasions, the Kremlin sought to mask its real fears and objectives. The U.S.S.R. would not dream of allowing its satellites to manufacture such weapons and has traditionally refrained from installing them outside its territory. (The recent deployment of Soviet tactical missiles in Eastern Europe appears to be a departure from this policy. But we still cannot be sure that the missiles located in East Germany actually are armed with nuclear warheads.)

But why should the Soviet Union seek its real goal in such a roundabout way? At the time few in the West, certainly no one in the United States or France, would have advocated an independent nuclear force for Germany.* Still, in the Kremlin's view—a view that cannot be denied a degree of logic—by stating your real fears you deliver a valuable bargaining chip to your adversary. Someone in Washington might be alert enough to ask, What is it worth to you to have Bonn banned from ever having a nuclear deterrent of its own? Would you in return, say, authorize free, internationally supervised elections in East Germany?

And why should the Soviet Union, then loudly proclaiming, indeed exaggerating, its advances and its superiority in the development of nuclear weapons, be so concerned about the distant possibility of West Germany's eventually acquiring what would be, at least in comparison with the United States, a very modest stockpile of nuclear weapons? The answer is that the Russians had learned to live with what at first was an American monopoly and as of 1957–1958 a still crushing superiority in such weapons. For all the past American incantations about massive retaliation, the Kremlin by 1957 had arrived at the realistic conclusion that it was unthinkable that the American democracy would launch a nuclear war without the most serious provocation, nor was Washington capable of exploiting its superiority in strategic arms even for political purposes.[4]

But the situation would be quite different if the "Bonn revanchists" got their hands on the dreaded weapons. The Federal Republic could then pressure or blackmail its Communist counterpart and thus trigger a catastrophic conflict between the two superpowers.

After the Rapacki Plan had been rejected by the West, Berlin became in the Kremlin's view the most efficacious tool for prying out of the United States and its allies what it most wanted—a nuclear-free Germany. The German peace treaty would have to contain ironclad guarantees against Bonn's ever acquiring nuclear arms. The U.S.S.R.

---

* In fact, under the conditions of its admission to NATO, Germany was banned from having such weapons.

sought additional benefits through the treaty: official recognition of the German Democratic Republic and the
elimination of West Berlin as an escape route for East
Germans. But in the Kremlin's view those were secondary
to the main purpose of the elaborate operation that began
with Khrushchev's celebrated ultimatum formally delivered to the Western powers on November 27, 1958. Its
gist was that if there were no peace treaty in six months,
there would be a blockade.

We do not have to rehearse a detailed story of the
four-year crisis. But what made it ironic is that the Berlin
game was interwoven with yet another complex Kremlin
gambit, equally misunderstood in the West. While he
was pressuring the United States on Germany, Khrushchev was slyly wooing this country, in the hope of reaching a Soviet-American understanding that might contain
China.

The Sino-Soviet conflict, long brewing beneath the
veneer of alliance and the allegedly unshakeable unity of
the two countries, burst into the open in 1959–1960. At
first many in the West took at face value the ideological
incantations in which the protagonists rationalized their
dispute. And, quite possibly, Moscow and Beijing were
sincere in anathematizing each other respectively as "re-
visionist" and "left-wing dogmatist and sectarian." There
was also the legacy of long-standing national hostility between the Russians and Chinese—muted for a while but
now, if anything, exacerbated by ideological propinquity.

But the main reason for the dispute was the Soviet
Union's frantic effort to prevent China from developing
its own nuclear deterrent and what turned out to be the
inflexible determination of Beijing to do so at any cost.
This motif comes out clearly from the bitter correspon-
dence beween the two Central Committees. Two quota-
tions are sufficient to demonstrate the partly dramatic,
partly comical tone of the dispute. Even in 1963, after
Khrushchev's elaborate schemes had collapsed in the
wake of the Cuban crisis, the Kremlin pled coyly with

Beijing that "China is as yet unprepared to produce nuclear weapons in quantity. Even if the People's Republic
of China were to produce two or three bombs, this would
not solve the question [of Chinese security] for it either,
but would bring about a great exhaustion of China's
economy." [5] Such Soviet solicitude failed to move Mao
& Co., who replied: "The Soviet Government . . . is in-
solent enough to say that we are able to criticize them
only because China enjoys the protection of Soviet nuclear weapons. Well then, leaders of the Soviet Union,
please continue to protect us awhile with your nuclear
weapons. We shall continue to criticize you . . ." [6]

But between 1959–1962 the Soviet leaders not only
pled with China, but actually schemed to persuade its
leadership to abandon or at least postpone its nuclear
ambitions. How could this be done, especially in view of
the now clearly and publicly worsening relations between
the two countries? It was probably Khrushchev himself
who conceived the ingenious idea of inducing or com-
pelling the United States to pay the price of Beijing's
abandonment of its nuclear pretensions. What he had in
mind emerges clearly from his statement at the Twenty-
First Congress in January 1959: "One can and must construct in the Far East and the whole Pacific Ocean area
a zone of peace and, first of all, a zone free of atomic
weapons." [7] The hint should have been clear: the Americans should pull out their nuclear arms from their Far
Eastern bases, which would imply that the U.S. should
withdraw its protection from Taiwan. As a quid pro quo,
China would give up its own effort to build the bomb.
At the time Chou En-lai, who was at the Congress, was
ready to second the plea for a Pacific nuclear-free zone,
or at least pretended to do so. His willingness was probably not unconnected with a concurrent Soviet pledge
to grant 5 billion rubles' worth of Soviet services and
goods to China, the most extensive package of economic
aid to be given thus far to the People's Republic by the
Kremlin.

It is dou·tful that much of the promised help was actually delivered, for within a few months Sino-Soviet relations reached the stage of open conflict. Beijing's long-standing suspicions of the erstwhile "elder brother" (as Mao referred to the U.S.S.R. in happier days) were heightened by Khrushchev's 1959 visit to the United States, where indeed the Soviet leader obliquely tried to raise the subject of China with Eisenhower, only to be met with the president's categorical refusal to discuss the question. Those suspicions were far from dispelled by the way Khrushchev followed his tour of the United States with a hurried trip to Beijing, where, one assumes, he attempted to explain to his hosts what he meant by hobnobbing with the imperialists, hailing Eisenhower as a constructive statesman, and inviting him to visit the U.S.S.R. During the next three years relations between Beijing and Moscow grew steadily worse, and their quarrel became known to the outside world, though few in the West yet appreciated how serious it was. Yet in the face of all that, the Russians continued to apply unremitting pressure on China to abandon its nuclear plans, their pleas and arguments meeting with continuous and eversharper rebuffs.[8]

The prospect that China would soon acquire the bomb terrified Washington as much as it did Moscow. The U.S.S.R., for all of the Kremlin's antics, was viewed by the Americans as a Communist power with which one could at least have a dialogue—witness Khrushchev's occasional amiability and the first signs of consumerism coming into its own in Soviet society. By contrast, the People's Republic, it was almost universally held, was ruled by fanatics who would brook no compromise with the capitalists, and who—witness Mao's explicit statement on the subject—viewed with equanimity the prospect of a nuclear war, since it was bound to bring a worldwide victory for socialism.

But again we cannot blame Khrushchev for not being explicit about his scheme of Soviet-American collusion in order to stop Beijing's nuclear development. In the first place, the Americans were completely incapable of conducting confidential negotiations on such a subject. Washington would have been incredulous—witness Eisenhower's statement when Khrushchev tried to broach the subject: "For the US, Red China has put itself beyond the pale"—or suspected a Soviet trick. And if the State Department finally became convinced of the seriousness of the Sino-Soviet dispute, the news of the U.S.S.R. seeking American assistance or cooperation would have undoubtedly leaked out, become the subject of congressional and media debate, scandalized the whole Communist world, and made Khrushchev's position vis-à-vis his Politburo colleagues even shakier than it already was. And how seriously would the West take Soviet threats about Berlin if fully apprised of how fearful the Russians were of China's developing even a rudimentary stock of nuclar weapons?

Khrushchev was not making much headway with the Americans, either as a bully or a suitor. We can in retrospect understand his dilemma. Should he press harder on West Berlin? Well, it was dangerous to carry the bluff beyond certain limits. Some of the more nervous members of the Kennedy administration would indeed not have been averse to tinkering with Berlin's status in order to calm the Russians, nor would the British, but Adenauer and De Gaulle held out firmly against any concessions. Anyway—and this was most exasperating to the Soviet leader—no one in the West seemed to comprehend that it was not the wretched city the Russians were really after.

As to a joint American-Soviet stance on China, the Soviets undoubtedly thought that they had hinted as broadly as possible when Andrei Gromyko declared at the Twenty-Second Party Congress in October 1961 that "our country places special importance on the character of the relations between the two giants—the Soviet Union and the United States. If those two countries united their efforts in the cause of peace, who would dare and who would be in a position to threaten peace? Nobody. *There is no such power in the world.*" [9] Yet nobody in Washington took note of those words. But how they must have resounded in Beijing! And indeed the Chinese delegation to the Congress walked out after lambasting Khrushchev (allegedly for his harsh language about Albania) and after Chou had delivered a violent attack on the United States, which this future architect of Sino-American rapprochement declared was the greatest enemy of world peace.

And then somebody in the Politburo, quite likely Khrushchev, had a brilliant idea: if Berlin was too sensitive a nerve of the Western system to be squeezed indefinitely, then there was another means by which you could force the United States to do what the Kremlin wanted. The Americans, once they saw what was up, would themselves understand that they should be sensible: the plan centered on Cuba.

Most postmortems on the Cuban missile crisis seldom dwell at length on the factors that impelled the Russians to provoke the crisis, which many observers still believe brought the two nations closest to nuclear war. The usual interpretation paraphrases Sir Edmund Hillary's famous statement that he chose to climb Mount Everest "because it is there." That is, the Russians tried to put missiles in Cuba because they wanted them there, close to the shores of the United States. As to the official Soviet explanations that the weapons were to be placed in Cuba to protect it from an impending American attack, the best comment came from Beijing on September 1, 1963: "Before the Soviet Union sent nuclear weapons into Cuba, there did not exist any danger of the US using nuclear weapons in the Caribbean ... It should be said if such a crisis did arise, it was as a result of the rash action of the Soviet leaders." [10]

Yet there is a great deal of evidence—circumstantial, to be sure—as to what the Russians were after in their Cuban gambit.[11] Preparations were made in great haste;

the Soviets proceeded in the late summer of 1962 to construct forty launch pads for medium- and intermediate-range missiles, without first erecting in Cuba the extensive antiaircraft missile network that would have made American detection of the pads from the air virtually impossible. And so they were to be ready, with some, at least, to have missiles deployed in them, before Khrushchev's visit to New York that was to take place in November, when he would address the United Nations. There he would announce the existence of the Cuban missile complex and pledge that the Soviets would dismantle it if the United States would agree to: (1) a German peace treaty of the kind delineated above; (2) a nuclear-free zone in the Pacific, with the Americans giving up their protection of Taiwan. After the initial shock, Khrushchev seems to have believed, the Americans would realize that what he proposed was really in their interest, too. As for the Chinese, for all their insistence on building their own bomb, they still might fall in with his plan, especially when they saw that he got the concessions not through negotiating with the capitalists, but by holding a gun to their head, so to speak.

Well, we know what actually did happen. The Soviet missiles were spotted by American aerial intelligence. There followed the U.S. "guarantee" (a euphemism for the naval blockade) of Cuba, as well as a threat of direct American action against the Soviet installations on the island. The U.S.S.R. then backed off from a confrontation by removing the missiles. Had Khrushchev's scheme been allowed to be completed, would he have achieved his objectives? It is impossible to say. It is natural that in their preoccupation about what to do about them Kennedy and his advisers could during those hectic October days give little thought to the question of why the Soviets sought to place missiles in Cuba. But subsequently it should not have been difficult to divine the Soviets' motivation, to notice, for example, how lo and behold the Berlin crisis vanished from the horizon once the Russians decided to terminate the Cuban adventure. And a correct reading of the Soviets' fears and intentions might well have saved American policy-makers a lot of future trouble. A realization of how serious the Moscow-Beijing conflict was should have instructed Washington not to obscure it by launching massive intervention in Vietnam.

The U.S. also should have questioned whether the Russians truly planned to install nuclear weapons in Cuba. Knowing the Soviets' aversion to deploying such weapons outside the U.S.S.R., even when under the full control of their military, it is reasonable to doubt that Moscow intended to equip the missiles with nuclear warheads. And that helps account for Castro's fury at the outcome of the Cuban crisis. Only then did he probably realize what the Russians were after and that it had nothing to do with protecting Cuba from the Americans. Perhaps the immediate aftermath of the crisis would have been a propitious time for Washington to try to wean Castro from Moscow.

IV

Even now, the Cuban missile crisis is far from being of merely historical interest. It is clear that, unlike Washington, the Kremlin has drawn from it a number of lessons that have influenced its policies to this very day. Khrushchev's techniques of bluffing and bullying were dropped as counterproductive and dangerous. In place of his strident tone and threats, the Kremlin would now pursue its goals of accommodation with the United States through more conventional diplomacy on the one hand, and through a rapid buildup of its arms, conventional as well as nuclear, on the other.* Helped immeasurably by

* Khrushchev tended to skimp on arms, believing that even a moderate-sized stick is sufficient to impress the capitalists, if you make loud noises about it.

America's predicament in Vietnam and its worldwide reverberations, this double-track policy had succeeded by 1972 in achieving at least half of what the Soviets had sought through their pyrotechnics between 1958 and 1962: de facto Western recognition of East Germany and Bonn by its subscribing to the Nuclear Non-Proliferation treaties and by acknowledging Poland's post–1945 frontiers, thus removing one of the two main sources of the Soviets' anxieties in the 1950s and 1960s.

As to the other one, détente in the Kremlin's view was supposed to lessen, inter alia, the political impact of the Sino-American rapprochement, and in fact it did so.

Looking at American policies in the 1960s and early 1970s, one must again note certain sins of omission and commission caused by this country's inability to discern the real motivations behind the Soviets' tactics. Was it wise for the West to offer Moscow the Federal Republic's nuclear abstinence, free of charge, so to speak, without intimating the need for a quid pro quo, such as the Russians' pressing their friends in Hanoi for a cease-fire in South Vietnam? When American civilian and military leaders decided in 1965 to freeze the number of American ICBMs despite the continuous and rapid Soviet buildup of the same, they undoubtedly had sound technical reasons. Yet they ignored the politico-psychological effect of the American quantitative inferiority in land-based strategic missiles as finally agreed on in SALT I and II. But the man in the street in Bonn, or for that matter in New York, could only conclude after the 1972 agreement that since the U.S.S.R. was allowed 1618 strategic land-missile launchers, as against 1054 for the U.S., the latter's nuclear umbrella over Western Europe had become very porous indeed, if it had not already blown away.

The political risks implicit in SALT I could have been mitigated if simultaneously with it NATO had brought its conventional armed forces up to the level of those of the Warsaw Pact, or if the problem of the balance of tactical nuclear weapons on the Continent had been addressed then, rather than in 1979. "What in Heaven's name does nuclear superiority mean?" Henry Kissinger asked rhetorically in 1972. It may mean very little in the event of a nuclear war between the two superpowers, or even as a deterrent to such a war, but nuclear superiority confers upon its possessor, especially if it happens to be an authoritarian state, enormous political advantages.

This recital of American misperceptions of the motivations behind Soviet policies could in some cases be matched by similar errors on the part of the Kremlin. But our task here is not to give grades to the diplomatic performance of the two systems or to pass moral judgment on their international behavior. America's main concern must be the devising of more effective ways of dealing with the Soviet Union. And the key to this lies partly in the ability of our policy-makers and our public opinion to perceive more clearly the real nature of what the Soviet Union fears, but also what it hopes for.

NOTES

1. Adam B. Ulam, *Expansion and Coexistence: Soviet Foreign Policy, 1917 to 1973*, 2nd ed. (New York, 1974), pp. 619–625, 661–675.
2. Arthur Schlesinger, Jr., *A Thousand Days* (Boston, 1965), p. 398.
3. Royal Institute on International Affairs, *Documents on International Affairs, 1957* (London, 1958), p. 408.
4. For the Rapacki Plan, see Ulam, *Expansion and Coexistence*, pp. 611–613.
5. Quoted in William E. Griffith, *The Sino-Soviet Rift* (Cambridge, Mass., 1965), p. 363.
6. Ibid., p. 371.
7. *The (Extraordinary) Twenty-First Congress of the Communist Party of the Soviet Union* (Moscow, 1959), p. 78.
8. A detailed account can be found in my *Expansion and Coexistence*, pp. 572–640, 656–667.
9. *Twenty-Second Congress of the Communist Party of the Soviet Union* II (Moscow, 1961), p. 343. My italics.
10. Quoted in Griffith, *Sino-Soviet Rift*, p. 669.
11. It is reviewed in my book *The Rivals: America and Russia Since World War II* (New York, 1971, 1976), pp. 299–340.

SOME LESSONS
OF THE PAST

Alexander Dallin

One may characterize Soviet-American relations as a combination of constants and variables. We are often concerned with the variables, and properly so. They include the changing balance of power, the role of nuclear weapons, the varying international and domestic contexts, crises, political actors, as well as the learning process of each superpower. The student of this relationship is also bound to be impressed by the weight of lasting continuities. These comprise not only the unchanging geopolitical settings but also the institutional framework and, perhaps most important, persistent elements in the American and the Soviet mind-sets and patterns of behavior. It is these constants and variables that make it possible to draw some lessons from the record of Soviet-American relations.

The establishment of diplomatic relations between the United States and the Soviet Union in November 1933 marked the end of a sixteen-year period in which official Russian-American relations were severed. Woodrow Wilson at first hailed the overthrow of the Russian tsar, which made it easier for the United States to enter the war on the Allied side. Then, after the Bolshevik takeover and withdrawal from the war in 1918, the Allies intervened to support the Whites against the Reds in the Russian civil war—a halfhearted and limited involvement that was doomed to fail.

The intervention provides a prime example of a peculiar American proclivity to meddle in Communist countries but not to follow a defined policy. With the Russian Revolution, the U.S. began a sequence of responses—some would say overreactions—to Communist takeovers that all too often substituted for real policy. Not that the miserably impoverished Soviet republic, after years of murderous war and in the throes of social chaos and political inexperience, constituted a threat to the United States or even to its European allies. If the initial aim of the intervention was to keep Russian troops fighting on the Eastern front, that reason vanished with the armistice of November 1918. What remained was an apparent decision to oust the Leninists from power. Yet two years later, with that effort a failure, the U.S. along with its allies pulled out, leaving the Bolsheviks in power, but refused to recognize their regime until Franklin D. Roosevelt entered the White House.

The history of American policy toward the Chinese Communists provides a rather similar pattern. In the 1940s, after the failure of the halfhearted American effort to keep the Maoists from coming to power, Washington—almost alone among the nations of the world—sought to ostracize the Beijing regime (at some cost to itself) until the normalization in the 1970s.

Soon after Fidel Castro seized power in Cuba, the United States attempted to oust his regime too, principally through the unfortunate 1961 Bay of Pigs operation but also, as we were to learn later, by an array of botched efforts to embarrass, assassinate, or otherwise dispose of him.

It was of course Vietnam that provided the most protracted and traumatic example not only of this country's apparent inability to tolerate the victory of a Communist regime but also of its unwillingness to commit the forces or invest the power needed to oust it (unless we are dealing with a Grenada). More recently the not-so-clandestine support of the Nicaraguan contras is another instance of the same itch.

I point to this repeated phenomenon because it illustrates two persistent and powerful tendencies in the American outlook. The first of these—apparently shared by leaders and the public—is an irrational fear of communism (which is blamed for everything from fluoridation, to the metric system, abortion, the oil crisis, and Ayatollah Khomeini). To point out this fear is in no sense to mute our own distaste for or disagreement with the Soviet system; it is to point to our persistent inability properly to determine where and how to commit U.S. prestige and resources, using limited resources in pursuit of attainable ends.

That question is of course also shaped by a second phenomenon that this pattern illustrates: the American public's seeming lack of staying power; its tendency not to take events thousands of miles away sufficiently seriously; its inability to make the requisite commitment to a sustained, long-term policy. I suspect that this proclivity reflects the combination of two mutually reinforcing elements—an old isolationism that dates back to the days of the frontier, and a new technological mentality of gadgets and gimmicks—that lead to the illusion that there are prompt solutions for every problem, a quick fix.

Most of the historical instances cited above pertain to regimes that constituted no serious threat to this country or to world peace. In contrast, the Soviet Union today does represent a serious military challenge. More often than not, however, the American reaction to that challenge is based on an exaggeration of Soviet power and Soviet control. This propensity was most obvious in the official U.S. misreading of the Sino-Soviet relationship, based as it was for so long on an almost theological belief that there could be no conflict among Communist parties and states. At earlier stages, Americans also exaggerated the conspiratorial elements in Bolshevism and its American adherents (at one time virtually every member of the American Communist Party, however naive and innocent of other ties, was seen as a traitor in the eyes of his or her fellow citizens). All these cases reflected a pervasive phenomenon: approaching the rival power with erroneous assumptions and expectations, some of which are discussed below.

As George Kennan has suggested, in international affairs there is no relationship of total antagonism or of total identity of interests.[1] Soviet-American relations have been and are bound to be at all times a mix of conflicting and cooperative elements—and it is precisely the changing mix that ought to be the central concern of policymakers. Tension is then a given, whatever our particular view of the balance of contributing factors. But the superpower relationship has been seriously complicated by numerous errors and failures of understanding on the part of both the Soviets and the Americans. In particular, each has erred in misreading the other's moves and misperceiving the other's intentions. Or when these were correctly perceived, they were packaged, overdramatized, and inflated so as to make political capital out of them at home and abroad.

I am far from arguing that this has been the whole story of Soviet-American tensions and conflicts; there would have been substantial difficulties in any event. But these unnecessary, subjective elements—perceptual and conceptual—have often aggravated the climate of hostility on both sides.

On the Western side, for example, one may recall the widespread expectation in 1945, in American government and media, that, after defeating Nazi Germany, the Red Army was poised to break through to the Atlantic; subsequent analyses have made a strong case that this need not have been a serious concern at that time. There was, behind the proclamation of the Truman Doctrine in 1947, the assumption that Stalin would fight to conquer Greece. Actually he was prepared to respect this part of the deal he had made with Britain, and, in fact, his refusal to support the Greek partisans caused further conflict with Tito, who at that time had no such reluctance. In 1950 the belief that the Korean war was the prelude to a Soviet attack on Japan proved to be unfounded, as did the view that the Soviets invaded Afghanistan in 1979 as a crucial step on the road to the Persian Gulf. In all these cases we adopted "worst case" hypotheses that turned out to be unwarranted and tended to warp our perceptions and invite counterproductive action.

The downing of the Korean jetliner in 1983 provided another example of misreading. The belief that the plane was shot down as a result of an explicit decision by the Kremlin appears to have been quite wide of the mark, as was the hypothesis that the Soviet military wanted to embarrass and perhaps oust Andropov.

Numerous examples from recent conflicts in places as widely scattered as Chad, Lebanon, Kampuchea, and Nicaragua come to mind to illustrate the widespread tendency in this country to see all problems abroad in East-West terms, as parts of a global, dichotomous confrontation, rather than on their own local or regional merits. On November 7, 1983 the *New York Times* quoted a senior official as saying: "Grenada, Beirut and the K.A.L. airliner all served to confirm in the President's mind his own view of the world, that there was a common thread to all these events and it all led back to Moscow."

If, in the pages that follow, I deal primarily with some

failings of American statesmanship and diplomacy, it is because my remarks are addressed to American readers: the Soviet list of miscues, misperceptions, and misapprehensions—while quite different—is probably just as long. The number of Soviet misreadings of world events would be even more substantial if we had access to the Kremlin files; in their case, we often do not know whether the policy-makers believe what they publicly say. Moscow's general view—or, better, ideological preconception —concerning the nature of imperialism and neoimperialism is a glaring example of a systematic distortion which, if taken at face value, qualifies the foreign policy of the United States and its allies—sight unseen—as "class based" and hence inimical. No less biased, for a long time, was the belief that the White House was but a tool of Wall Street (a good example of an axiom that has almost vanished over the course of time).

More concretely, in 1927 Soviet leaders claimed to see a coming Western attack on the Soviet Union; during the Depression they expected the United States and Great Britain to fight as the only way out for the major capitalist states (war among capitalist states being considered ultimately inevitable, and military expenditures and establishments then being viewed largely as a device to reduce economic stagnation and unemployment—another instance of a set of misperceptions that have been revised long since).

Stalin's foreign-policy misjudgments and misperceptions are numerous. In the mid-twenties he did not want to believe that the Chinese nationalists would turn on their Communist allies; in fact, he persisted in his refusal to acknowledge their "betrayal" (and his error of judgment) long after the evidence was in. Similarly, in 1941 he refused to credit the copious intelligence that Hitler was about to attack the U.S.S.R. (apparently because it would prove that his policy of a Nazi-Soviet deal was fundamentally mistaken). Later he insisted that Gandhi was a stooge of British imperialism and the whole decolonization that followed the Second World War was a sham.

It remains an open question whether any leading Soviet foreign-policy officials believed, and therefore acted on, the trumped-up charges that the prominent Bolshevik victims of Stalinist terror—Marshal Tukhachevsky, Nikolai Bukharin, Leon Trotsky—were in fact agents of foreign powers, or that the East European Communist leaders purged in 1949–1952 were part of a CIA-Titoist-Zionist-Gestapo conspiracy.

Nikita Khrushchev miscalculated the Western reaction to his threats over Berlin and to his tactics at the United Nations; they were soon exposed as little more than bluster and bluff. His moves, which precipitated the Cuban missile crisis in October 1962, were as dangerous a case of misjudging the United States—both its intelligence capability and its determined response to the imminent emplacement of nuclear missiles in Cuba—as any, before or since.

The Helsinki Accord of 1975 is another example, inasmuch as it has boomeranged for Moscow by giving the West a legitimate handle on human rights in the Soviet bloc. Afghanistan may be another case of Soviet miscalculation, of cost and time required for the Soviet Union to achieve effective control, as well as of the invasion's impact abroad.

But history will surely conclude that the most monumental blunder was to sacrifice détente with the United States in the 1970s for an almost unrestrained Soviet military buildup and an extension of Soviet influence in the Third World—often costly, dubious, and transient. I do not believe that Moscow ever made an explicit decision regarding this priority, and in fact it tends to explain the failure of détente in very different terms, but whether by inadvertence and incompetence or by choice and deliberation, that is what Soviet behavior and Soviet policy choices amounted to.

Even this brief enumeration suggests that Soviet learning—however slow and imperfect—led to the gradual abandonment of some of the grossest and most "ideological" misperceptions, while more recent errors of judgment in Moscow often have reflected incompetence, personality traits, or a failure to consider elusive or inconvenient variables. By contrast, while United States knowledge and understanding of the Soviet Union have increased dramatically, and while here too some of the cruder forms of hysteria—such as locating "the threat" of alleged Soviet agents among American citizens—have been mercifully abandoned, there has been a remarkable persistence of certain assumptions and expectations which, in my judgment, are dangerously misleading.

What are some of the American fallacies or oversimplifications that we encounter about Soviet motives and behavior?

Soviet conduct as an ideology in power. No single factor suffices to explain what Moscow is up to. While much of the orthodox rhetoric of Marxism-Leninism has remained, as has the ritual use of doctrine as a state religion, Soviet outlook and policy have been a changing mix resulting from the encounter of prior assumptions and expectations with reality as the Soviets have perceived it. They had expected a much simpler world, one that conformed to the Marxian categories of good and evil, friend and foe, progressive and reactionary—a world that naturally would become transformed in the way their doctrine mandated. It turned out that there was no good fit between belief and experience. What we find is, over time, an increasingly attenuated use of orthodox verbiage and categories.

The canons of Marxism-Leninism have been less and less useful for coping with a complex and confusing world in which Soviet leaders must make decisions concerning questions—ICBMs, computers, outer space, the Sino-Soviet dispute, and garbage collection—that deal with categories or phenomena that Marx and Lenin never had an opportunity to consider. Instead, Soviet leaders find themselves increasingly consulting technical, military, scientific, and area specialists. This does not mean that they can—or want to—shed what has been called their operational code, including their deeply ingrained assumptions about the way the world is spinning and how to deal with problems as they arise.[2] But whatever the continuing verbiage, the removal of some ideological constraints in the conduct of day-to-day business does give them more flexibility to see more things and do more things. To be sure, the range of policy options is usually narrower than in the United States; nevertheless, there has been an unfolding of significant policy debates in Moscow. While no doubt political indoctrination continues to produce a contingent of "true believers," the more apt comparison, it has been suggested, is with Sunday sermons or Fourth-of-July oratory which the listener believes but which usually fails to produce behavior congruent with the values he or she has just heard.

Soviet foreign policy as world conquest for communism. This formula is sometimes a corollary of the assumption that Marxism-Leninism plays a pervasive role in Soviet motivation. In my view, there is no ideological imperative for the Soviet Union to expand or to seek conflict abroad. There have been periods when it has not expanded and has not suffered particularly ill effects, as was essentially true from 1921 to 1939, and again in the years following Stalin's death in 1953. And whenever it has expanded, Soviet advances abroad have not been in the service of a doctrine, whatever its rhetoric. If anything, this rhetoric may in fact have done it a disservice by leading foreign observers to take its arcane arguments at face value.

Ideological formulas have of course been used since 1917 to explain a multitude of sins: ideology can justify going it alone or making alliances; it can justify militant and conciliatory policies, peaceful and violent ones. To argue that the Soviet regime needs an enemy to maintain a mobilizational atmosphere and permit a primitive dichotomy of us against them, however, is not to say that Moscow needs to expand or to attack. To say that the image of international relations dominant in Moscow is a conflict model is not to make any specific prediction about Soviet foreign-policy behavior. To say that the Soviet Union would like to see the United States and other capitalist powers collapse, and that it asserts such a collapse to be ultimately inevitable, is not to say very much either. After all, most of us would like to see the Soviet system and the Soviet bloc disintegrate, too. The question on both sides is: At what cost? By what means? When and how? And if ideology can justify action now, it can equally well rationalize waiting. The long-range utopian vision, in other words, has no single set of necessary operational implications.

There is also a more sophisticated variant of this proposition, which argues that the extension of Soviet sway, or Communist control, provides legitimation for the regime and its official creed among the Soviet population and perhaps among comrades abroad. No doubt Soviet ideologues do indeed use the growing scope or power of the "socialist world system" to validate Leninist beliefs and expectations. It is even likely that Soviet decision-makers welcome the extension of Soviet influence abroad for this among other reasons. But there is no basis for believing that decisions concerning commitments abroad, notably using force or taking more than minimal risks— in Ethiopia, Afghanistan, or Syria—are significantly shaped by the perceived need to manufacture fodder for such legitimation.

Soviet policy as the implementation of a master plan. There is in fact no master plan for Soviet practitioners to follow, no blueprint that would tell Soviet officials what to do next, no "timetable of aggressiveness." We give them far too much credit for possessing a grand design and for the "scientific" planning of their foreign policy.

If half a century ago there was a Marxist-Leninist "itinerary of world revolution," it surely was not expected to pass through Tirana, Luanda, Grenada, Addis Ababa, Kabul, Phnom Penh, or even Havana. But "world revolution" was a phrase current at a time when Soviet reliance was placed on history as the inevitable ally of communism and on Communist parties abroad as the instrument of history. Since those days Soviet faith in the workings of inevitability manifestly has receded—for good reason —as has Moscow's confidence in the ability of its comrades abroad to do anything right—again, for good reason. This meant a fundamental reorientation to a reliance on building up the Soviet state. A later reorientation saw a shift to the primacy of military competition with the West, in a distinctly un-Marxian fashion. Such shifts in Soviet strategy underscore the conclusion that there has been no master plan; at most there has been a sequence of miniplans, one by one abandoned or revised.

Far more characteristic has been a Soviet skill of exploiting opportunities abroad—opportunities created at times with Soviet help but largely by forces beyond their control.

Soviet foreign policy as tsarism in overalls. One of the most pernicious approaches to Soviet behavior, I believe, is one that starts by positing that "once a Russian, always a Russian," and "every country gets the government it deserves." This pessimistic determinism argues that Russians are inherently militaristic, cunning, deceitful, untrustworthy, and that all this cannot and will not change—that Russia's past determines its future—one that is, and is bound to remain, at odds with the United States.

Despite the widespread tendency to interpret Soviet behavior abroad as the extension of prerevolutionary Russian practice, I see little merit in invoking historical antecedents—the ghosts of Genghis Khan, Byzantine Emperors, Ivan the Terrible, or Peter the Great—to explain Soviet policy, just as I see little use in invoking the Inquisition, the abuses of the French Revolution, or the reign of Savonarola or of Oliver Cromwell in considering the political behavior of their successors, centuries later.

Historical determinism is as treacherous a guide as economic or technological determinism, and I hope we would have rejected the argument in 1945 that Germany and Japan could never be democracies or, had we lived in 1788, that France would always remain an absolute monarchy. History is not merely a repetition of what came before, or else it would be a lot more predictable and even more boring than some of our students insist it is.

It goes without saying that a people's collective experience does help shape later memories and values, and that the study not only of Russian history but also of Soviet political culture—however elusive the concept—is an important and legitimate endeavor, as relevant and significant in the Soviet case as it is in others.

Soviet foreign policy as adventurism. Contrary to widespread impression, Soviet foreign policy typically has not been rash, but rather committed to a fairly low level of risk-taking. That level may have gone up as Soviet capabilities have increased over time, but the record of Soviet involvement abroad shows that Moscow has generally opted for actions that have not carried with them the danger of big-power conflict. For instance, it avoided an open conflict with China even when relations were at their worst, and it shied away from confrontation with the United States, whether in the Middle East or in the Caribbean. It has been cautious even with regard to Yugoslavia, Iran, and Finland (though its attack on the latter in the Winter War of 1939–1940 represents a prime example of a mistaken Soviet assumption that a small country such as Finland, abandoned by friends and allies, would not possibly fight the Soviet colossus, especially after Lithuania, Latvia, and Estonia had just folded under similar pressure).

It is true that the Soviet Union need no longer narrowly circumscribe its activities in support of its clients in Vietnam, Cuba, and Zaire, as it had to in the early 1960s, because of technological limitations: meanwhile it has acquired a global reach—merchant marine, civil and military aviation, submarines and aircraft carriers, and heavy intercontinental missiles. However, it is not clear that Moscow is now prepared to take risks higher than before.

The only conflicts into which Moscow has stumbled (as distinguished from wars in which the Soviet Union was attacked) have been those where it misread the signs or miscalculated the prospects (as in the Finnish or Korean war). While this may be small comfort, the lesson for us is to make absolutely clear and credible what American commitments and intentions are in order to minimize the chances of such Soviet misconceptions.

Soviet plans to wage and win nuclear war. In line with the preference for risk avoidance, the evidence is overwhelmingly that, contrary to certain alarmists,[3] the Soviet Union is not planning to provoke a nuclear showdown between the superpowers. Its chiefs do not exclude the possibility that a nuclear confrontation will occur, or that an accident or conventional war—say, in Europe—could escalate into a nuclear exchange, but they are certainly not itching for it.

It is the role of the military in all countries to be ready to fight and to meet a broad range of possible contingencies and scenarios. Soviet training and deployments certainly envisage such a prospect; it would be irresponsible for the Soviet decision-makers, and the military command in particular, to fail to do so. But it is misleading to draw the conclusion from Soviet training manuals and civil-defense bunkers that the Kremlin expects to initiate a nuclear attack and benefit from it. What Soviet leader would gamble that enough Soviet ICBMs could hit enough targets more than seven thousand miles away, and enough Soviet forces and assets could escape retaliation to make the gamble worthwhile? Soviet leaders, too, have an increasingly vivid sense of what nuclear devastation means (as well as a keen appreciation of technological limitations and imperfections).

None of this implies that the Soviet view (military or civilian) of the role of force in international affairs is the same as that of the U.S., or that Soviet war-fighting doctrines, training, and procurement do not reveal distinct and at times troublesome features. Moreover, Moscow, like other capitals, is of course keenly aware of the political uses of military power and not at all reluctant to resort to them. But that is a far cry from planning to win an all-out nuclear war.[4]

Soviet policy as the product of totalitarian unanimity. The American government has assumed that on the Soviet side we are dealing with a "unitary rational actor." All too often divergences in Soviet pronouncements have been dismissed as trivial, exceptional, or even orchestrated to deceive us. Yet to be able to explain Soviet policy outcomes it is essential to get a good sense for Soviet political life with its bargaining, its deals and trade-offs, its jockeying for influence and power, and its efforts to maximize political resources and develop influential constituencies.

The failure of Western observers to recognize both the variety of bureaucratic interests and the diversity in values, attitudes, and policy preferences within the Soviet elite has constituted a major blind spot in our understanding of Soviet affairs. Because of Soviet secrecy and U.S. ideological blinders, we have underestimated the degree of uncertainty and the tensions among Soviet policy-makers, their foreign-affairs analysts and advisers.

The Soviet Union is a conservative system that neither lives up to images of superhuman achievement nor conforms to innuendos of subhuman conspiracy. We are dealing with a gray mass of officials who have not come up with fresh answers to the complex questions they were supposed to address. I believe that the Soviet leadership and those who brief it are not nearly as sure of their answers as they claim to be and as we often believe, whether on energy policy or on relations with China or the United States, on arms control or on increasing efficiency in their economy.

Further, there is strong evidence that there is a fundamental ambivalence in Moscow about the outside world, and all sides in the debate can at all times invoke a strain of the Leninist legacy that supports their views. There are the old tensions between diplomacy and revolution, commitment and restraint, optimism and pessimism about the outside world; between what George Kennan once called the desire to enjoy and the desire to destroy; between the Soviet self-image as the chosen, riding the crest of the wave of history, and a sense of inferiority, of being encircled, of being behind, of being used and abused.

Since the Stalin days there has been a cleavage between those who advocate greater interaction abroad and those who favor greater isolation and self-reliance. In recent years, the attractions of stabilizing the international scene have competed with the commitment to promote "progressive" changes abroad. Many of these tensions follow from a protracted and often reluctant attempt at adaptation—of squaring theory with practice, of adjusting mind-sets and beliefs to a world that invariably turns out to be more complex, more intractable, more recalcitrant, more varied and unexpected than the Soviets were taught to believe. Even if there is a consensus on many core values within the Soviet elite, the remaining differences —both on policy objectives and on how to implement them—are important for us to understand.

Compensatory expansionism. There has been another misleading hypothesis making the rounds, both in Washington and among academics, to explain Soviet activism abroad: the notion that the Kremlin seeks successes and perhaps victorious little wars as a way of compensating for problems at home. Such a notion would reconcile elegantly the contradiction between alarm at Soviet aggressiveness and the emphasis on Soviet domestic weaknesses —from declining economic-growth rates to increasing alcoholism and pandemic corruption.

But the notion does not stand up to close scrutiny. At moments of greatest domestic stress (as far back as 1921, 1930, 1937, and 1953) Soviet foreign policy has invariably shifted to conciliation, not aggressiveness. Moreover, Soviet leaders today do not see their country in a state of crisis requiring such a compensatory policy. Nor do they advertise their military (nor, to some extent, their economic) involvement abroad—say in Ethiopia or Afghanistan—in a fashion calculated to appeal to domestic audiences. On the contrary, it is typically underplayed.

Finally, attention must be drawn to a pervasive confusion among the American public but especially in the government and the media: the view of communism as a threat. Communism as a belief system is scarcely the menace that it is so often made out to be. Ideas and beliefs alone are never a security threat. Moreover, they cannot be combated by organized power, let alone armed forces. Nor does rule by a Communist party necessarily constitute a danger to American security: Hungary, Yugoslavia, and Mongolia are cases in point and suggest both the varying meanings that *communism* has come to assume in different countries and at different times, and the crucial fact that what is decisive in determining whether a given political system represents a real or potential threat to American security is the combination of its rulers' intentions and capabilities.

This is not the place to discuss whether, or to what extent, the Soviet leadership constitutes such a threat today. But if it does, in full or in part, it is Soviet power—

and above all, military power—and not communism that is the source of the threat.

Constraints in the conduct of foreign policy, in both the United States and the Soviet Union, stem from the political institutions, the political environment, as well as the mind-sets and perceptions of the actors in domestic politics. In regard to the United States this subject has been studied and commented on at length. All too frequently foreign-policy decisions are tailored to appeal to special interest groups and public opinion—or, on other occasions, are frustrated by appeals to (or the intervention of) lobbies—whether ethnic, ideological, or economic. The Jackson-Vanik Amendment of 1974, which in effect made Soviet-American trade a hostage of changes in Soviet human-rights practices, and the Senate's failure to ratify the SALT II treaty in 1979, after it was negotiated over seven years with the support of three successive administrations, exemplify political intervention in the foreign-policy process, in large measure because of special pleading from the outside and the presumed electoral appeal of such a posture. A close eye on electoral opinion certainly influenced the decision of the 1980 Reagan electoral staff to make anti-Sovietism a major campaign issue, as well as the administration's reversal from an initial hostility to arms-control negotiations to the initiation of START talks in 1981, and the grain deal with the Soviet Union concluded as the new Cold War escalated in 1983.

The grandstanding of incumbents and critics alike is a matter of record. The media have helped oversimplify and overdramatize issues. No less familiar—and no less important—is the tug of war between the executive and legislative branches. The four-year cycle of administrations means that in practice there is little, if any, collective memory, and every new team—usually lacking in

continuity and previous experience—tends to reinvent
the wheel, convinced that it must develop a new approach. The first six months of any new administration
are typically a time of inaction while incumbents are
"getting on top of issues," and the last year is effectively
spent with one eye (if not both) on the coming election.
Bureaucratic infighting frequently reduces policy making
to contests of clout and produces negotiated and often
self-contradictory and self-defeating language instead
of coherent policies. Participants in Soviet-American
arms control talks have remarked privately that reaching agreement among American agencies and actors
is at least as difficult as negotiating with the Russians.

Comparable domestic factors are not absent from Soviet foreign-policy making, even though they are a good
deal less salient. While it is essential to avoid naive
mirror-imaging by projecting American institutions and
collective attitudes onto the Soviet scene, there are indeed some universal factors impinging on all systems.
Thus, just as is true over here, information, policy alter-
natives and preferences, and perceptions are filtered
through the mind-sets of Soviet leaders and their advisers.
Though in a somewhat different way from U.S. practice,
Soviet bureaucratic politics plays a major role. In addition, there are constraints and pressures specific to Soviet
political culture and institutions. Resource constraints
powerfully affect military and foreign-policy decisions.
The culture requires all officials never to be seen as de-
viating, changing, doubting, or erring. Rival interests—
military, economic, and ideological—must be satisfied
or paid off. At both ends the decision process can be
painfully slow and devious.

Neither in Moscow nor in Washington do the best
and the brightest often rise to the top. But, while on the
Soviet side the level of competence slowly has been rising—among foreign-affairs experts consulted by the policy-makers generally, and among specialists on American
affairs, in particular—on our side the input of qualified

experts into the government's analysis of Soviet affairs and policy formulation appears to have been declining, after a dramatic improvement during the quarter-century after World War II. This is a troubling trend.

Referring some years ago to the domestic setting in which policy toward the Soviet Union is made, Merle Fainsod, then the dean of Soviet studies in this country, wrote:

However great may be [Soviet difficulties in embarking on a genuine improvement of relations with the U.S.], a part of the trouble lies within ourselves. We are a nation torn by conflicting pressures, wavering between hopes for peace and fear of communism, weary of foreign entanglements and yet fearful of abandoning them, more confident in our means than clear about our purposes, sure of our good intentions and frustrated when others do not recognize them, accustomed to victory and feeling betrayed when we must settle for less, believing that every problem must have a solution and baffled when none is forthcoming, impatent with long drawn-out negotiations, yet compelled to learn how to make creative use of them if we wish to survive.[5]

Twenty years later his words are as valid and pertinent as they were then.

The direction of future trends in Soviet policy and society is uncertain, not only because we do not know enough about them but also because the Soviet leaders themselves do not, and cannot, know what answers they themselves or their successors will find for the many problems they face. Policy choices are increasingly difficult to make in a situation in which measures that promote economic growth and efficiency are apt to be opposed by bureaucratic interests suspicious of all change that may threaten their vested interests. Under conditions of scarcity and stringency, demands for capital, labor, and resources for investment and consumption must compete with the frequently higher priority of security needs. Political coalitions in the elite appear to make possible little more than token reforms while frustrating attempts at more fundamental change. The relevant policy community in Moscow may often be divided among competing—and in all cases unsatisfactory—options advocated by rival interests and groups. It would take a strong leader to overcome the inertia and resistance, even if the corruption, the anomie, and the loss of faith could be repaired from above; yet at best such a leader would require substantial time to establish himself with such authority, and while there is some nostalgia for a strong man in power, there are also powerful forces poised to prevent the reemergence of a dictator.

Under these conditions, policy preferences and choices, especially in foreign affairs, may well be influenced in significant ways by variables beyond Soviet control, including perceived threats and opportunities abroad. Among these variables are United States conduct and capabilities. And it is precisely this open-endedness of future Soviet conduct that makes it imperative for American policy to show an uncommon measure of subtlety and flexibility—traits not always associated with our foreign policy.

While we should respond to undesirable Soviet behavior with countermeasures—if only to disprove the argument by irresponsible Soviet hawks that Moscow may proceed on a forward policy with impunity—we equally must be prepared to provide positive reward and recognition for Soviet behavior that we welcome and support. We must, in other words, seek to use our assets to reinforce Soviet groups that have a stake in getting along with the United States.

But such flexibility must not come at the expense of clarity and consistency of policy. Few things in recent years have so upset and confused both our friends and our adversaries as the zigzags and reversals of American policy—not only from one administration to another but especially within each—and the multiple tongues with which each administration has spoken.

One of Kissinger's deputies, Helmut Sonnenfeldt, wrote some years ago (before they reversed course, in effect abandoning their earlier efforts at Soviet-American détente) that "we have entered an era in which the United States and the external world generally can seek increasingly to draw the Soviet Union into the constraints and disciplines but also the advantages of the international system." [6] He should not so readily have given up on this insight. How to steer the Soviets toward a more responsible and restrained role in foreign affairs is a problem that defies simple solutions but urgently needs to be pondered.

The United States can and inevitably does influence Soviet behavior and Soviet perceptions and priorities. Even if it can do so only marginally, at times it may provide precisely the crucial margin to affect decisions. But to use this potential effectively is no simple matter. Surely gimmickry and improvisation will do no good if the broader context is one of misunderstandings; policy and behavior have to be a coherent and consistent whole. A precondition for influencing Soviet behavior is knowing and studying the subject and if need be reexamining our own assumptions in the process; optimal U.S. influence requires, first, an openness to learning and, second, a patient and skillful use of our vast arsenal of instrumentalities, resources, and techniques.

Whether we like it or not the Soviet Union is here to stay. Its behavior is at times bound to be mysterious, frustrating, and infuriating. Yet we have no alternative but to live on the same planet. As John Van Oudenaren has ably shown, the choice for American policy-makers has been between termination of the Soviet-American conflict and conflict-management. And since termination—either by a first nuclear strike or by surrender/accommodation—is unthinkable or unacceptable, managing Soviet-American relations remains a must. [7]

If the two superpowers differ on many matters, they are also bound to share some interests, the first of which is survival in a nuclear world. That fact ought to dictate both the parameters of our behavior and part of the agenda for early Soviet-American negotiations.

The United States has shouldered global responsibilities, and it must honor them. Its credibility must by all means be kept up. But there are limits to what is proper and prudent for this country to do in regard to the "Soviet problem," as to everything else. International politics too is the art of the possible. This is an invitation neither to passivity nor to weakness, but to a statesmanlike selection of issues and places over which to become involved, whether with the Soviet Union or with other powers.

If we could reduce the vast zone of misconceptions, trim the impediments of domestic pressures and constraints, make fuller use of our experts, and have a better-informed and more sensitive public, and if Moscow could be made to respond in kind, Soviet-American relations would be vastly more manageable, stable, and secure. Then full attention could be paid to the real issues that divide our countries.

NOTES

1. Cf. George F. Kennan, "The United States and the Soviet Union," *Foreign Affairs*," July 1977.
2. The term "operational code," originally coined by Nathan Leites (*The Operational Code of the Politburo* [McGraw-Hill, 1951]), has been reintroduced with a somewhat different and far more valuable meaning by Alexander George. See his "The 'Operational Code' . . ." *International Studies Quarterly*, Vol. 13, No. 2 (June 1969).
3. For instance, Richard Pipes, "Why the Soviet Union Thinks It Can Fight and Win a Nuclear War," *Commentary*, July 1977; also Joseph Douglas and Amoretta Hoeber, *Soviet Strategy for Nuclear War* (Stanford: Hoover Institution Press, 1980).

4. Cf. David Holloway, *The Soviet Union and the Arms Race* (New Haven: Yale University Press, 1983), and his "Military Power and Political Purpose in Soviet Policy," *Daedalus*, Fall 1980, pp. 13–30. For another view, see Fritz Ermarth, "Contrasts in American and Soviet Strategic Thought," *International Security*, Fall 1978.
5. American Philosophical Society, *Proceedings*, Vol. 108 (October 20, 1964), pp. 429–36.
6. Eric Hoffman and Frederic Fleron, eds., *The Conduct of Soviet Foreign Policy*, 2d ed. (Aldine Press, 1980).
7. John Van Oudenaren, *U.S. Leadership Perceptions of the Soviet Problem* (Rand Corporation Doc. R–2843–NA, 1982).

HOW WE SEE
THE SOVIETS

Robert Dallek

I have been a student of American foreign policy for twenty years, and I have never ceased to marvel at the distortions and illusions shaping U.S. actions in foreign affairs. This is not a uniquely American trait; other nations and governments have also been prone to misperceptions and unrealism in international relations. Moreover, the American record includes its share of victories, with economic, political, and military actions enlarging the country's wealth and power and preserving it from devastating conflict. The vast territorial acquisitions in the nineteenth century, the climb to superpower status, and the avoidance of nuclear war through a policy of deterrence in the twentieth century represent impressive achievements. Nevertheless, a substantial record of foreign misadventures—utopian aims in World Wars I and II, the denial of transparent threats between the wars, and exaggerated fears of a monolithic Communist danger since 1945—suggests that there is something in the American approach to overseas affairs that makes us particularly vulnerable to misunderstandings about the world beyond our borders.

This difficulty may be ascribed to a number of views we hold: our traditional assumption that, like most Americans, nations respect the rule of law; our conviction, growing out of our national experience with free security and limited need for power to ensure our safety, that high-minded principles could be the determining force in international affairs; and our impulse to use external events to promote internal political control. But beyond, or perhaps beneath, all these concepts there has been an indifference to foreign affairs and an absorption with domestic concerns that has blinded us to what the outside world is really like. For most Americans, the international scene has been a remote, ill-defined sphere onto which they projected foreign policies expressing unresolved internal tensions or relieving tormenting domestic concerns. As political scientist Stanley Hoffman has stated, "the roots of America's troubles abroad are at home: in the American bundle of ignorance, illusions, habits and fears, and in our intractable political system." [1]

George Kennan has emphasized how much this parochialism has shaped American thinking about the Soviet Union. He sees the motivations for U.S. policy toward Moscow as

primarily subjective, not objective, in origin. They have represented for the most part, not reactions to the nature of a certain external phenomenon (the Soviet regime), but rather the reflections of emotional and political impulses making themselves felt on the internal American scene ... The record of American policy toward the Soviet Union over the six-and-a-half decades of the existence of that body politic gives the impression that it was not really the nature of any external problem that concerned us but rather something we were anxious to prove to ourselves, about ourselves. [2]

The proposition has been demonstrated by the fact that shifts in official U.S. attitudes and policies relating to the Soviet Union have apparently had little, if anything, to do with "changes in the nature of the problem that country has presented for American statesmanship." The Soviet government we refused to recognize in the twenties was little different from the one we established official relations with in the thirties. The Stalin regime of 1939 that outraged us by signing the Nazi-Soviet Pact "was precisely the same as that in which we came to discern so many virtues during the war. This latter, in its turn, was no different from the one that we discovered, at the end of the 1940s, to be a great danger to us and to the free world in general." Similarly, the alternations in American policy since 1953 from Cold War evangelism to détente and back to anti-Soviet messianism have had far less to do with changes in the post-Stalin Soviet structure of power than with changes in American mood and attitude.

None of the above is meant to suggest that American reactions to the Soviets have been strictly the product of a preoccupation with domestic affairs. On the contrary, American policy-makers, especially since 1945, have been attentive to Soviet actions in every part of the globe. The Truman Doctrine, the Marshall Plan, and the NATO agreement in the late forties, for example, all rested in large measure on realistic perceptions of the Soviet challenge to American national security. Likewise, American defense chiefs have monitored the buildup of Moscow's military strength over the years and have generally made realistic assessments of how the United States could counter the Soviet threat. But this realism has been no guarantee against misperception and distortion in dealing with the U.S.S.R. In our approach to the Soviets, realism and illusion have always gone hand in hand. The fact that I have much less to say about the former than the latter is not meant to suggest that realism played no role in our Soviet policy; it obviously did. But if we are to expand our understanding of Soviet-American difficulties, it seems essential to focus on how we contributed to these problems rather than on what we are doing right. In a nuclear age, when a misreading of Soviet aims can lead to global destruction, we need, above all, to probe the roots of American misconceptions about the U.S.S.R.

As Kennan suggests, an impulse to project deep-seated feelings about ourselves has been in large part at the core of American dealings with Russia. When objective differences have strained Soviet-American relations, it has not been enough for Americans to look at the realities driving the two sides apart; we have also needed to see a Communist ogre intent upon and capable of destroying the "American way of life." This reaction says more about American uncertainty over the effectiveness and durability of our institutions than about the realities of Soviet aims and power. At times, when many Americans have been particularly unhappy with developments in the United States, they have used Moscow as a symbol or stand-in for those values with which they are at odds in our domestic life. Similarly, when circumstances have drawn the U.S. and the U.S.S.R. together, it has not been enough for Americans to view the improved relationship as the consequence of national security needs; they have also viewed it as a demonstration of the triumph of American customs and ideas. Warmer Soviet feelings for the United States suggest to numerous Americans not so much that they need something from us, but that they want to become like us. This distortion reflects an irrational need to reinforce a belief in the virtue of our system.

The period of nonrecognition between 1918 and 1933 is an example of how internal absorptions colored and distorted our perceptions of the Soviets. Relations with the revolutionary Soviet government after World War I were understandably tense. Petrograd's withdrawal from the fighting, the separate peace treaty with Germany signed at Brest-Litovsk in 1918, and rhetoric about world revolution created antagonisms in the United States that could not be easily shunted aside. In the context of these actions, even the most realistic and politically adept American statesman would have had difficulty establishing normal relations with the new Russian government immediately after 1918.

What is most striking about these difficulties, however, is not that they held us back from the normalization of relations, but that in conjunction with domestic problems they became a basis for wildly exaggerated fears about the new Soviet regime. American participation in the Allied intervention in Siberia in the summer of 1918 was rationalized as an effort to strike against German prisoners of war who had been armed by the Bolsheviks to destroy Czecho-Slovak forces. Although there was no significant German force operating in Russia, numerous Americans insisted they saw a Russo-German alliance that would threaten to invade the United States and Canada through Alaska. In 1918, the *New York Times* portrayed this "German-Russian Empire" as "the most frightful menace conceivable." In 1919–1920 the successful Bolshevik uprising in Russia and the spread of revolution across Europe and of strikes and anarchist bombings across America touched off a Red Scare in the United States. Feeling menaced by alien radicals, millions of Americans enthusiastically supported arbitrary arrests and deportations by the federal government. For the rest of the decade Americans continued to oppose recognition of the Soviet regime because it was so uncivilized: it failed to pay its debts, allow religious worship, honor agreements, and renounce international revolution. At bottom, the historian Christopher Lasch has pointed out, Americans "assumed that the United States could have relations only with a regime which shared its own attitudes and assumptions about the world."

The important point here, I believe, is that a Soviet state that was so at odds with American institutions and beliefs intensified existing American fears about the state of this nation. The failure of progressivism in the years 1900–1920 to achieve its stated goals of greater democracy, law, justice, morality, and, above all, a sense of shared national harmony and order left many Americans in the twenties with doubts about the survival of traditional habits. The growth of special-interest politics during the decade—cities vying with small towns, Drys with Wets, Protestants with Catholics, laborers with corporations, farmers with businessmen, fundamentalists with intellectuals, government with free enterprise—raised fears of domestic strife in the United States. These concerns made Americans highly sensitive to Soviet challenges to their national customs and provoked reactions out of proportion to the actual threat.[3]

Just as the mood of insecurity about national institutions in the twenties made us excessively fearful of a Soviet government that was so different from our own, we seized upon the convergence of Soviet-American interests in the forties to reinforce a renewed sense of national harmony by depicting the Soviet Union as becoming just like the United States. The New Deal in the thirties and involvement in World War II in 1941 created a revived sense of American unity. During the thirties the United States underwent a "consolidation of transportation, communications, and mass media, resulting in a country-wide standardization" that affected "everything from manufacturing codes and farming practices to soap operas. Homogenization of such regional distinctions as language, dress and custom proceeded rapidly, a result not only of technological advances but also of federal application of national policies and programs to local areas." By the mid-1940s, Americans were "talking alike, dressing alike, and perhaps thinking alike as never before." In religion, education, literature, and historical scholarship, the impulse was toward shared values and a national sense of purpose.

The thirties and forties also saw a push in the United States for a "federation or commonwealth of nationalities." The objective was "to recognize the diversity of national strains in America and to seek to create a harmony among them." The hope was that from the many varieties of peoples in America, one would emerge. In his 1943 best-selling book, *One World*, Wendell Willkie, the Republican presidential candidate in 1940, expressed a similar view: "Our nation is composed of no one race, faith, or cultural heritage. It is a grouping of some thirty peoples possessing varying religious concepts, philosophies, and historical backgrounds. They are linked together by their confidence in our democratic institutions as expressed in the Declaration of Independence and guaranteed by the Constitution." America had reached a high level of civilization, Willkie concluded, because of "the ability of peoples of varying beliefs and of different racial extractions to live side by side... with common understanding, respect, and helpfulness." [4]

During the war, when the U.S. and the U.S.S.R. shared a common desire to destroy Nazism, American opinion-molders of the Left, Right, and center voiced the conviction that Soviet-American friendship would continue indefinitely because the Soviets were becoming more and more like Americans. In perhaps the most famous wartime expression of this view, *Life* magazine, a conservative publication, declared in March 1943 that the Russians were "one hell of a people... [who] to a remarkable degree... look like Americans, dress like Americans and think like Americans." The NKVD was "a national police similar to the FBI." The following year the *New York Times* declared it no misrepresentation "to say that Marxian thinking in Soviet Russia is out. The capitalist system, better described as the competitive system, is back." Other commentators described Russia as no longer "Communistic," pointing to a steady movement away from a "narrow Marxian ideology in the direction of ideas that we can call, in very broad terms, democratic." In the summer of 1943, conservative congressman John Rankin of Mississippi described communism as so un-

popular in the Soviet Union that it was being run out of
the country. In 1944 Herbert Hoover told the Republican nominating convention that Russia was no longer
truly Communist.[5]

No one gave clearer expression to this view in the
United States than Willkie. In *One World*, he described
a trip to the Soviet Union in the fall of 1942, showing
him that there were many more similarities between the
United States and Russia than he had previously thought.
The grain crops running to the horizon reminded one of
Texas; the irrigated valley near Tashkent looked like
Southern California; the stately manors along the Volga
were like the great houses on the banks of the Hudson. A
visit to the small stone house of a collective-farm manager evoked memories of a prosperous farmhouse in the
United States. There was "a hearty hospitality, with
much laughing good humor," and the manager's wife
urged Willkie "to eat as I have been urged many times
in Indiana farmhouses." Yakutsk in Siberia was like a
western American town a generation ago. It reminded
Willkie of "our own early and expanding days—especially the hearty, simple tastes, the not too subtle attitudes of mind, the tremendous vitality." It was like "El-
wood [Indiana] when I was a boy." The leader of the
Republic of Yakutsk was a thirty-seven-year-old who
"talked like a California real-estate salesman" and once
more reminded Willkie of earlier days in America when
men were "chiefly interested in getting things done."
Above all, the American visitor found a democratic Russia, where the country was fighting a people's war and
men and women enjoyed equality of opportunity and a
chance to improve their lives. Stalin, their leader, was "a
simple man, with no affectations or poses . . . If you continue to educate the Russian people," Willkie told him,
". . . you'll educate yourself out of a job." Stalin was
highly amused.

Roosevelt encouraged this view of Soviet-American ties
after the Teheran Conference in December 1943. "I got

along fine with Marshal Stalin," he told the nation in a
fireside chat. "I believe he is truly representative of the
heart and soul of Russia; and I believe that we are going
to get along very well with him and the Russian people
—very well indeed." What were "your personal impressions of Marshal Stalin?" a reporter asked the president
after Teheran. "We had many excellent talks," Roosevelt
replied, which would "make for excellent relations in the
future." Another reporter asked: "What type would you
call him? Is he dour?" The president answered: "I would
call him something like me . . . a realist." [6]

What explains these wartime illusions about Soviet
Russia? Awareness of the fact that many Russians were
dying in a cause with which Americans could thoroughly
identify is part of the answer. With Russians giving their
lives in a struggle that directly served U.S. national survival, it was easy for Americans to lose sight of differences
between the two countries. Yet this alone seems inadequate in explaining the extent to which educated people
fell into this mood. Wartime polls indicated that a favorable attitude toward Russia was much more common
among well-educated, prosperous Americans than among
less-educated, low-income groups. This suggests that well-
off Americans who identified most strongly with the
country found it easy to imagine that the whole world
wished to be like them or to imitate what existed in the
United States. Russia abandoning communism for capitalism and democracy made transparent good sense to
those convinced that their nation was a model that peoples all over the globe would wish to emulate. Henry
Luce expressed the idea perfectly in a 1942 *Life* article:

Because America alone among the nations of the earth was
founded on ideas which transcend class and caste and racial
and occupational differences, America alone can provide the
pattern for the future. Because America stands for a system
wherein many groups, however diverse, are united under a
system of laws and faiths that enables them to live peace-

fully together, American experience is the key to the future
... America must be the elder brother of nations in the
brotherhood of man.[7]

After World War II, when the disappearance of a common enemy allowed the reemergence of existing differences between the U.S. and the U.S.S.R., numerous
Americans refused to acknowledge that the wartime alliance had been a marriage of convenience that would
not outlive the resurfacing of natural antagonisms between the two powers. Instead, they felt terribly betrayed
by postwar Soviet actions and by some American policy-
makers, who were seen as either consciously or unwit-
tingly collaborating with Moscow in a reach for worldwide control. At a time of rapid change in American life,
when the U.S. largely abandoned its traditions of relative
free security and military and political isolation and great
numbers of Americans seethed with tension and anxiety
over their "relationships to people, to production and
consumption," they used the Cold War, in historian
Richard Hofstadter's words, "as a constant source of recriminations about our moral and material failure ... as
a kind of spiritual wrestling match with the minions of
absolute evil." The visceral, evangelistic anticommunism
of these Americans was a way of demanding recognition
for their values and their importance in American life.
The objective struggle against communism abroad interested them less than their battle with it at home, where
they boosted their self-esteem by seeing themselves as
defenders of conventional American verities against Communist subversion.

These domestic tensions registered forcefully on the
Eisenhower-Dulles policy toward Moscow. Convinced
that the United States was locked in an apocalyptic struggle with the Soviet Union, Eisenhower described the
contest as one between freedom and slavery, lightness
and dark, good and evil. Dulles denied all possibility of a
"permanent reconciliation," saying, "this is an irrecon-

cilable conflict." Calling for the "liberation" of areas
under communist control, the Republican party platform
of 1952 promised to replace "the negative, futile and immoral policy of 'containment' " under Truman with the
"contagious, liberating influences which are inherent in
freedom." [8]

Throughout the fifties, this Eisenhower-Dulles orthodoxy persisted almost unchanged. Although Stalin died
in March 1953 and his successors largely pursued a policy
of "peaceful coexistence and competition" with the
United States during the remainder of the decade, the
Eisenhower administration never broke with its assumptions about the Soviet communist threat, showing itself
less responsive to external realities than one might expect
from leaders as familiar with the world as the president
and his secretary of state. The reverses in foreign affairs
of the late forties and early fifties, the Communist victory in China, the Soviet detonation of the atomic bomb,
the failure to defeat Chinese forces in Korea and unify
that country, contributed to frustrations and fears that
help explain the single-minded approach to meeting the
Soviet Communist challenge. But by the mid- and late
fifties these reverses no longer seemed sufficient to account for this enduring orthodoxy. Instead, one needs to
consider the possibility that, throughout Eisenhower's
term, policy toward the Soviets had as much to do with
the mood at home as with events abroad. Indeed, as in
the twenties, the national state of uncertainty over domestic affairs moved many Americans to pursue a rhetorical crusade against a nation whose political and economic
system represented a standing challenge to their values.

While the Eisenhower administration, of course, never
followed through on "liberation" and practiced a more
flexible strategy in its dealings with Moscow than its rhetoric suggested, it nevertheless insisted on Soviet conver-
sion to American standards. In 1953, after Moscow called
for direct talks with the United States about disputed
problems, Eisenhower and Dulles rejected the proposal

unless they had prior assurances that the Soviets would accept a number of American demands: a peace treaty with Austria, freedom for thousands of prisoners of war held from World War II, a Germany united on the basis of free and secret elections, full independence for Eastern European nations, and arms-limitation agreements. The administration was asking Soviet conformity to American political assumptions as a precondition for a dialogue. From Moscow's perspective, a dialogue on that basis would have played havoc with Russian security. But this hardly registered on the administration or on most Americans, who warmly backed the president's demands. The objective, at bottom, was less to enter into talks than to insist that the Soviets become more like Americans.

Despite this impulse, by the summer of 1955 Eisenhower felt compelled to meet with the Soviets. A number of developments at home and abroad, especially the acquisition of the H-bomb by both sides, created the feeling, as Eisenhower expressed it, that "there is just no real alternative to peace" and that discussions would have to be tried. But the goal of converting rather than accommodating the Soviets remained intact. What he wanted to talk about, Eisenhower later recorded, was "the plight of enslaved peoples behind the Iron Curtain, and the aims of international Communism," or "the basic purposes of the international Communist conspiracy." Preliminary discussions offered him "little hope of a truly changed attitude on the part of the Soviets" toward these subjects. Moreover, he prepared himself to counter what his advisers saw as the chief Soviet goal at the conference: "a recognition by the Western powers of the 'moral and social equality' of the Soviet Union." Since this would strengthen the Soviet hold on its satellites and encourage neutralism, American planners urged the president to avoid social gatherings, where he would be photographed with the Russian leaders, and to maintain "an austere countenance" when he was with them before the cameras. As if to emphasize the moral and

social differences between the two sides, Eisenhower addressed the nation before he left for Geneva on "the
cardinal religious concepts which form the very core of
our democratic society." He asked all Americans, on the
next Sabbath, to "crowd their places of worship" to ask
for help in achieving peace. "This would demonstrate to
all mankind that we maintained great armaments only
because we must. Our armaments did not reflect the way
we wanted to live; they merely reflected the way we had
to live." The message was clear: America, the morally
superior nation, would go to Geneva hoping, with God's
help, to convert the Russians to American ways of peace.
Nothing less would suffice. The three major goals the
administration set for itself at Geneva were:

A unified Germany, militarized and safely within NATO;
European security, by which was meant fewer Soviet troops
stationed in central Europe and a relaxed Soviet grip on the
countries of eastern Europe; and a leveling and control of
armaments, with the United States retaining an unchallenged
superiority of and supervision over nuclear weapons. The
likelihood of Soviet concurrence in any of these was nil.[9]

The principal Eisenhower proposal on disarmament—
"open skies"—underscores the point. In a dramatic gesture calculated to demonstrate American devotion to
arms reduction and peace, the president suggested an exchange of military blueprints of armed forces followed
by regular and frequent aerial inspections to verify their
accuracy. "I only wish that God would give me some
means of convincing you of our sincerity and loyalty in
making this proposal," he declared. It might indeed have
required an act of Providence. Since the Russians already
knew "the location of most of our installations," Eisenhower told his advisers, "mutual agreements for such
overflights would undoubtedly benefit us more than the
Russians, because we know very little about their installations." Described by critics as a gimmick, a ploy by

Cold Warriors practicing psychological warfare, "open skies" also evoked Premier Nikita Khrushchev's wrath: "A very transparent espionage device," he told Eisenhower. "You could hardly expect us to take this seriously."

But the president had little difficulty rationalizing his maneuver. In his view—and that of most Americans, who gave him a 79 percent approval rating on his return from Geneva—he was dealing with either "communist zealots or power-mad dictators." In either case, they were unbending in their ambition for world power and their hostility to the United States. At Geneva the Russians "drank little and smiled much . . . Obviously planned and rehearsed," Eisenhower later observed, "their efforts to ingratiate were carried out with precision and mechanical perfection." Failing to induce the five Soviet leaders at the conference "to reveal their true purposes and ideas" during a gathering at his villa, the president nevertheless found it "a useful evening in that I saw that the implacability of this quintet in a social situation would certainly be encountered in ensuing conferences and we would have to shape our own tactics accordingly." General Georgi Zhukov, his old comrade-in-arms from World War II, was no longer the man he had been in 1945. Subdued, worried looking, and unsmiling, Zhukov impressed the president as well trained for a performance. "He spoke as if he was repeating a lesson that had been drilled into him . . . My old friend was carrying out orders of his superiors." As for Khrushchev, he was a "ruthless and highly ambitious politician" who cared "nothing for the future happiness of the people of the world—only for their regimented employment to fulfill the Communist concept of world destiny."

Eisenhower's observations were more revealing of U.S. attitudes than of Russian realities. From the American perspective, the Soviets were not to be bargained with but converted and won over to the virtues of free elections, independence, disarmament, and peace. Since Soviet intransigence seemed to make this impossible, the next best thing was to demonstrate American moral superiority to peoples everywhere—the principal function, for example, of "open skies." In some abstract way, Eisenhower played out the dominant mood in the United States. Intolerant of dissent or anything that could be described as un-American, the country wanted conformity at home and abroad. "We are all items in a national supermarket," declared one commentator on the American scene, "categorized, processed, labeled, priced, and readied for merchandising." As a result of fundamental economic and social changes, which made social popularity and acceptance more desirable traits than individualism, Americans took comfort in self-evident truths to which moral people everywhere would subscribe. Just as the nation had no patience with domestic divisions or factional strife, it saw no room for negotiation with opponents of the U.S. credo overseas. If the Soviets would not abide by American standards of proper behavior in international affairs, they, like nonconformists in the United States, were to be ostracized. Eisenhower's moral indignation toward the Soviets at Geneva for refusing to accede to American ideas echoed the moral recriminations toward dissenting opinion in the United States. Conformity and orthodoxy at home set the standard for U.S. policy overseas.[10]

This compulsive need to see the Soviets in domestic terms continued to dominate administration thinking in its second term. A second meeting between Eisenhower and Khrushchev in 1959 illustrates the point. In September the premier traveled to the United States, where he urged the necessity of a détente between the two nations. "Many Americans nursed serious misgivings" about Khrushchev's visit, Eisenhower recorded in his memoirs. "Some of the more vociferous were those who opposed any kind of contact with the Soviets, but others were persons of standing, not only in political life, but also in business, labor, and the clergy." The exchange of visits, the president assured one of the critics, "implied no hint

of a surrender." He was true to his word. When Khrushchev privately declared that the Soviet Union "did not
want war" and his conviction that "we [Americans] realized this fact," Eisenhower "agreed that there was no
future in mutual suicide, but remarked that the attitudes
shown at the latest meeting of the foreign ministers gave
a contrary impression." The "big obstacle on the American side" in the way of better relations, he perceptively
told the premier, "was a matter of national psychology,"
the need for Americans to believe that Soviet communism did not stand for the destruction of the United
States. Eisenhower himself bore out this remark. Though
Khrushchev agreed "to remove any suggestion of a time
limit within which he would sign a Soviet-East German
peace treaty" and though "a crisis over Berlin had been
averted without the surrender of any Western rights,"
the president refused to acknowledge that a new positive
mood had taken hold in Soviet-American relations. Khrushchev later "talked about 'the spirit of Camp David,' "
but Eisenhower "never used" the term or thought it
"valid." [11]

There is no question that Soviet Russia posed a threat
to the United States in the fifties and that the Eisenhower administration needed to defend American and
allied interests against excessive Soviet gains. But the
more important question about the period is why the
United States so consistently overreacted to that threat,
why the administration repeatedly saw Russian defensive-
ness as aggressive and uniformly turned Asian, Latin, and
Middle Eastern nationalism into Communist attacks on
American security. Part of the answer is that foreign affairs reflected the uncertainty dominating the decade.
Foreign policy was as much a way to express and rationalize a troubled society at home as a means to defend
the national interest abroad. With large numbers of
second-generation Americans experiencing a shift in economic and social status and great pressures to conform or
assert their identities as 100 percent American, it was

difficult for the country to pay close attention to external realities. In an atmosphere of national dislocation, foreign policy became a symbolic politics in which the world outside eased cultural conflicts within.

Even the Nixon-Kissinger dealings with the Soviets in the early seventies, the most realistic assessment of the Soviet Union by any administration in the postwar era, was not immune to the impulse to use Moscow to confirm our self-worth to ourselves. In pursuing détente with the Soviets, Nixon and Kissinger made much of the idea that they have a distinctive system and that they would maintain a separate identity. During the summit talks in Moscow in 1972, Nixon declared: "There must be room in this world for two great nations with different systems to live together and work together." Yet in discussing Vietnam with Soviet Premier Alexei Kosygin, the supposedly unsentimental, realistic Nixon stated: "Our goal is the same as yours. We are not trying to impose a settlement or a government on anybody."

For all Nixon's talk of differences, he could not resist the belief that the Russian leaders were just like him and other self-made Americans. "Brezhnev's office was the same room in which I had first met Khrushchev, thirteen years before," Nixon recalls in his memoirs. "I was sure that neither of us, standing shoulder to shoulder in the kitchen at the American exhibition thirteen years before, had imagined that we would one day be meeting at the summit as leaders of our countries." And Nixon told Kissinger:

We constantly misjudge the Russians because we judge them by their manners, etc., and we do not look beyond to see what kind of character and strength they really have. Anybody who gets to the top of the Communist hierarchy and stays at the top has to have a great deal of political ability and a great deal of toughness. All three of the Soviet leaders have this in spades, and Brezhnev in particular ... Like an American labor leader, he has what it takes ...

He also reminded Nixon of "a big Irish labor boss, or perhaps an analogy to Mayor Daley [of Chicago] would be more in order." But whomever he called to mind, he was the consummate self-made man with "a great deal of animal magnetism and drive which comes through whenever you meet him." [12]

No American government in the post–World War II era better illustrates the American propensity to use the Soviet Union to deal with domestic concerns than the Reagan administration. The organizing principle of Ronald Reagan's defense and foreign policies is anti-Sovietism—the need to confront and overcome the Soviet Communist danger in every part of the globe. Reagan shares the legitimate concern, expressed by all American presidents since 1945, with the threat to America and its allies from a totalitarian Soviet Union hostile to their way of life. Unlike his predecessors, however, Reagan sees almost no room for reasonable compromise with the Soviets and looks forward to the day when the West "will transcend Communism. We will not bother to denounce it," he said in a 1981 speech. "We'll dismiss it as a sad, bizarre chapter in human history whose last pages are even now being written."

What explains this anti-Soviet evangelism? Reagan's rhetoric and actions suggest that in a fundamental way it is a symbolic protest against the state of his own nation. His anti-Soviet attitude arises as much from inner conservative tensions about government authority and social change as from any realistic understanding of Soviet aims and capabilities. For Ronald Reagan, the world outside the United States is little more than an extension of the world within; the struggle to defend freedom and morality abroad is a more intense version of the battle to preserve these virtues at home. In the eyes of Reagan and other conservatives, the communism of the Soviet Union represents the end point, the logical culmination of dangerous currents that they see running so powerfully in America—big government, atheism, and relaxed moral standards. More broadly, as *Harper's* editor Lewis H.

Lapham wrote, America sees in the Soviet Union "what it most fears in itself . . . Americans portray [the U.S.S.R.] as a monolithic prison, a dull and confined place where nobody is safe and nobody is free." It is a land of stereotyped commissars and peasants, of "cruel ideologues bent on world domination" and hapless victims of a repressive government. Through these caricatures, Lapham concluded, "Americans aim at the targets of their own despotism," at those modern ideas and institutions that threaten to make old habits like rugged individualism and family values out of date.[13]

Reagan's portrait of Soviet communism, unchanged since the 1950s, is of a ruthless, power-mad system bent on the creation of a "one-world Communist state" in which individuals and the traditional Western concepts of freedom and morality count for nothing. Children growing up under Russian communism, Reagan said during his 1980 presidential campaign, are taught that people's "only importance is [their] contribution to the state —that they exist only for that purpose, and that there is no God, they are just an accident of nature . . . This is why they have no respect for human life, for the dignity of an individual." At his first press conference in January 1981, the president made similar observations when asked if détente with the Kremlin were possible. Soviet Communist leaders had repeatedly affirmed their desire for

world revolution and a one-world Socialist or Communist state . . . Now, as long as they do that and as long as they, at the same time, have openly and publicly declared that the only morality they recognize is what will further their cause, meaning they reserve unto themselves the right to commit any crime, to lie, to cheat, in order to attain that, and that is moral, not immoral, and we operate on a different set of standards I think when you do business with them, even at a détente, you keep that in mind.[14]

Reagan's description of Soviet communism is plausible. It has been a repressive, totalitarian regime at home and has exhibited an evangelistic fervor for influence abroad, especially when its national security is involved, as in Eastern Europe, where it has established a kind of empire. Other American presidents and foreign policy-makers have used similar language to describe the Soviets, but unlike Reagan they have recognized that Moscow is also a self-interested nation-state that is open to a certain amount of give-and-take in world affairs. Reagan has been much less willing to accept this as a fact of international politics because his depiction of the Soviet Union is less a balanced, realistic view of its internal conditions and external aims than an amalgam of conservative complaints about conditions in the United States. When Reagan speaks of Soviet statism, of Communist indifference to personal freedom and the dignity of the individual, he is referring as much to conservative perceptions of recent trends in America as to the state of Russian affairs. After World War II, Reagan told an interviewer in 1980:

When the Soviet Union—when it looked as if the world might go into a thousand years of darkness—Pope Pius XII said, "The American people have a great genius and capacity for performing great and generous deeds. Into the hands of America, God has placed an afflicted mankind." I want to see, I want to help get us back to those fiercely independent Americans, those people that can do those great deeds, and I've seen them robbed of their independence, I've seen them become more and more dependent on government because of these great social reforms.

To Reagan and a certain group of conservatives, there are striking similarities between a Communist Russia and a welfare-state America that they see as abandoning its traditional spirit of rugged individualism. For Reagan and some Christian fundamentalists, anticommunism is also a crusade to restore traditional assumptions about God, family, and country to a central place in American life. The mission for a conservative president, Reagan believes, is to limit the size and power of government and revive conventional verities at home while repelling and if possible destroying communist power abroad.[15]

Americans who make anticommunism an extension of their fight for greater personal freedom at home also derive a sense of status from their militancy against the Soviets abroad. Indeed, fundamentalists and libertarians use the crusade against communism as a demonstration of their Americanism and their importance in preserving the nation. Superpatriotism, pride in country, pride in the flag, pride in America's men and women in uniform are central elements of this Cold War fundamentalism. Emotional patriotism has been a stock ingredient of Reagan's speeches for years. His inaugural address celebrated America's heroes and gave recognition to a fallen American soldier in World War I who cheerfully made the supreme sacrifice for his country. This nationalism is also meant to compel an overseas revival of respect for America, a renewed deference to the United States by friend and foe. For its staunchest advocates, the aim of this resurgent nationalism is to assure that other nations will no longer defy or ignore America or, perhaps more to the point, ignore it. The deference these superpatriots demand from other countries differs little from what they ask of their fellow citizens at home.[16]

Despite occasional expressions of concern to negotiate differences with Moscow, Reagan remains largely devoted to the anti-Soviet evangelism with which he began his term. In March 1983, for example, he told a group of Christian evangelists in Florida that America's conflict with the Soviet Union was a "struggle between right and wrong, good and evil." He called Soviet Russia an "evil empire" and totalitarian states "the focus of evil in the modern world." Reagan coupled his attack on the Soviets with renewed pledges to seek constitutional amendments permitting prayer in public schools and banning abortions.[17] The connection seems reasonably clear: Soviet power and influence must be combated, not simply because they represent a threat to the United States, but because they are the embodiment—the symbol—of trends toward more government control and relaxed family values that conservatives deplore. Reagan and his principal advisers have little energy to focus on local realities abroad. Their attention is largely fixed on challenges to their values from leftists around the world. The exaggerated Soviet threat—a Moscow pushing its evil purposes in every corner of the globe—is the product of the conservatives' obsession with defeating unsettling trends and bolstering their own self-esteem.

No one sensitive to the difficulties involved in the national shift to modern currents of behavior can deny the usefulness of illusions in easing America's way through the twentieth century. Nor should one overlook the fact that all nations in one degree or another base their foreign policies on domestic forces that have little to do with external actualities. Nevertheless, the United States, with its isolationist past and its history of free security, seems particularly prone to this sort of unrealism. At the same time, however, it is clear that many Americans are not comfortable with this distortion. President Reagan's excessive anti-Sovietism, for example, has created a backlash in American opinion and forced him to soften his rhetoric and to be more accommodating toward Moscow. This hardly suggests that the United States is about to enter a golden era of realism in foreign affairs, but it indicates that Americans may be more inclined than ever to recognize that using outside events in even limited ways for internal purposes will neither solve domestic problems nor provide the security and peace we yearn for in world affairs.

NOTES

1. Stanley Hoffman, "In Search of A Foreign Policy," *New York Review of Books*, September 29, 1983, p. 55.
2. George F. Kennan, "America's Unstable Soviet Policy," in *The Nuclear Delusion: Soviet-American Relations in the Atomic Age* (New York, 1983), pp. 228–230.

3. For domestic influences on American foreign policy in the post–World War I years, see Robert Dallek, *The American Style of Foreign Policy: Cultural Politics and Foreign Affairs* (New York, 1983), chapter 4. For the Lasch quote and a description of the response to the Soviet Union in 1918–1919, see Christopher Lasch, *The American Liberals and the Russian Revolution* (New York, 1972), pp. 107–112, 217–218.

4. For how domestic unity influenced wartime attitudes toward the world, see Dallek, *American Style of Foreign Policy*, chapter 5. The country's consolidation is described in Charles C. Alexander, *Nationalism in American Thought, 1930–1945* (Chicago, 1969), especially pp. viii–ix, 86; and Richard Weiss, "Ethnicity and Reform: Minorities and the Ambience of the Depression Years," *Journal of American History*, Vol. LXVI (December 1979), pp. 566–585. For the Willkie quotes, see Wendell Willkie, *One World* (New York, 1943), pp. 192–194.

5. For these comments, see John L. Gaddis, *The U.S. and the Origins of the Cold War, 1941–1947* New York, 1972), pp. 38–39, 57–58.

6. Willkie, *One World*, chapters 4–5, especially pp. 69–70, 73, 83–84, 92, 97–98. Robert Dallek, *Franklin D. Roosevelt and American Foreign Policy, 1932–1945* (New York, 1979), p. 439.

7. Gaddis, *U.S. and Origins of the Cold War*, p. 46. Ralph B. Levering, *American Opinion and the Russian Alliance, 1939–1945* (Chapel Hill, N.C., 1976), pp. 141–45, 155–556.

8. For domestic influences on foreign policy during the Truman and Eisenhower years, see Dallek, *American Style of Foreign Policy*, chapters 6–7. The Hofstadter quote is in Richard Hofstadter, *The Paranoid Style in American Politics* (New York, 1965), pp. 80–81.

9. Dwight D. Eisenhower, *The White House Years: Mandate for Change, 1953–1956* (New York, 1963), pp. 506–510. Peter Lyon, *Eisenhower: Portrait of the Hero* (Boston, 1974), p. 656.

10. Lyon, *Eisenhower*, pp. 653, 660–65. Eisenhower, *Mandate for Change*, pp. 517–525.

11. Townsend Hoopes, *The Devil and John Foster Dulles* (Boston, 1973), pp. 493–496. Dwight D. Eisenhower, *The White House Years: Waging Peace, 1956–1961* (New York, 1965), pp. 435–436, 446–449.

12. Richard M. Nixon, *RN: The Memoirs of Richard Nixon* (New York, 1978), pp. 609–611, 613–614, 619–620.

13. On the Reagan defense and foreign policies, see Robert Dallek, *Ronald Reagan: The Politics of Symbolism* (Cambridge, Mass., 1984), chapters 5–6. For the quotes, see the *New York Times*, May 18, 1981, II, p. 7; the *Los Angeles Times*, December 6, 1982, II, p. 9.
14. The quotes are in Robert Scheer, *With Enough Shovels: Reagan, Bush and Nuclear War* (New York, 1982), pp. 42, 148–49; and the *New York Times*, January 30, 1981, p. A10.
15. Scheer, *With Enough Shovels*, p. 260.
16. For the inaugural speech, see the *New York Times*, January 21, 1981, p. A1.
17. *Los Angeles Times*, March 9, 1983, p. 6.

HOW THE SOVIETS
SEE US

Hans Rogger

In the summer of 1866, Assistant Secretary of the Navy
Gustavus Fox and units of the U.S. Fleet sailed to Russia
to congratulate her people and emperor on his escape
from an assassin's bullet. Their visit was the high point
of a diplomatic and emotional rapprochement between
two peoples who, if they were alike in little else, were
matched in the intensity and demonstrativeness of their
feelings for each other. Their mutual delight on that occasion can only be described as an infatuation. In St.
Petersburg and Moscow, American sailors became as
much of a rage as Russian seamen had been in San Francisco and New York where their captains, fearing compli-
cations with Britain and France, had sought shelter during
the Civil War and where their country was hailed as the
Union's friend and ally in a dark hour.

In the port of Kronstadt, a Countess Apraksina, boarding the monitor *Miantonomoh*, wore a costume whose

bodice was of a blue material spangled with stars, a skirt of alternate stripes of red and white, and a sailor hat bearing the name of the vessel that was acclaimed as a symbol of America's technical genius. America's institutions had become almost as fashionable as her colors, and many a toast was drunk to them by ministers, merchants, and municipal councilors who drew parallels with their own reformed organs of local government and justice, with the sacrifices they too had made for freedom and equality, and with their own near loss of a beloved leader who had freed the serfs almost two years before Lincoln had emancipated the slaves.[1]

One of the speakers was Mikhail Pogodin, the conservative historian and spokesman of official nationalism who in 1837 had written of America as tainted by her illegitimate birth in revolution—not a state, but a trading company that had, to be sure, grown rich but would never create anything of great national or universal significance. Pogodin's contempt for the huckster state was quite forgotten as he told the Americans that sympathy for them was increased by history, by a common European heritage, and by a similarity of institutions.

As regards institutions, the United States is a republic and Russia an absolute monarchy, but here as well as on the map, extremes meet. In the Russian absolute monarchy, there is a representative stream that flows uninterruptedly throughout its history. As regards the forms, all of them have lost much of their original meaning, and our guests have justly . . . remarked that under our form of government one may progress; and they now hear . . . that the Russians, thanks to our gracious Emperor . . . may express their ideas and reason as freely as people do in New York.[2]

The guest of honor did indeed receive such impressions as Pogodin described. If they were not altogether wrong —Alexander II was doing much to reform the nation's internal life—they were uncritical to the point of blindness and inspired by the euphoria of the moment. What

the Americans heard and saw was also colored by a measure of self-congratulation, as in the presentation by Fox
to a Russian mayor ("elected by universal suffrage") of
an American flag; it represented, that worthy was told,
the ideas the tsar was promulgating. "This Emperor is
evidently impregnated with the democratic ideals of the
age and instead of waiting to be driven he is leading these
ideas amongst a people that looks up to him almost with
adoration." [3]

Alexander was no Lincoln, and Karakozov, who had
made an attempt on Alexander's life, no Booth, but a
revolutionary student who was hanged, as the socialist
Alexander Herzen acidly remarked in his London exile,
to the strains of Yankee Doodle playing for the departing
Americans. Nor did Russia attain universal suffrage for
another fifty-one years. But like many Americans and
Russians then and since, Fox took a temporary community of interest for a permanent identity of values and
beliefs. In an even more impressive exercise of wishful
thinking, so did Russia's leading liberal newspaper when
it proclaimed that the warm reception given the Americans was animated by the common ideals of humanity
and progress that both nations had so recently affirmed.[4]

The conservative editor Mikhail Katkov was not carried away by the general enthusiasm. Although, like his
government, he had favored the North—rebellion in the
South and revolt in Poland were seen as comparable instances of sectionalism and secession—and rhapsodized
about the *Miantonomoh* and the brilliant prospects
awaiting the two peoples, his ardor was reserved for the
benefits Russian diplomacy would derive from their
association. "An alliance between the United States and
Russia," he wrote in 1866, "can be based only on mutual
interest and contains, therefore, neither self-delusion nor
deceit." In 1869 he became disturbed over dangerous competition in the grain trade and warned that relations
would suffer from the sale of Alaska and geographical
proximity. A few years later, one of the merchants who

had spoken at the Moscow banquet complained that
"happy America has been fleecing us for cotton for fifty
years and extracting billions from us." [5]

For the Slavophile publicist Ivan Aksakov the Civil
War confirmed the inevitability of coercion in a nation
that was bound only by a counting of individual wills and
a fragile contract. Federalism, its very essence voluntary
agreement, had been violated in a conflict that in the
dimensions of its horror was truly worthy of America—
an orgy of killing with the most advanced tools of civilization. Coercion and cruelty were of the very nature of
war and the state, but in this, as in so much else, the
Americans had gone to absurd lengths. Without a deep
religious faith, without a true nationality, without art and
philosophy, they had added little to the treasury of mankind except machines and their products and still lived
off the spiritual capital of Europe. "When these traditions disappear, a truly American nation will be formed,
a state without faith, ethical foundations, and ideals;
either it will perish from the unbridled passion of selfishness and the unbelief of the individual or it will become
a terrible despotism of the New World." [6]

However skeptical Herzen was of the facile parallels
drawn at the time of Fox's visit, he could not resist pointing out that he had long foretold America and Russia's
meeting and becoming traveling companions for the future. Again he stressed their affinities and their freedom
from ancient prejudices, only to ask whether the "most
fateful antinomy" of Western history was not now expressed in the atomization of American society on one
hand and the collectivism of the Russian peasant com-
mune on the other. "*America fara dà se,*" he told Polish
comrades in 1867. Strong, crude, powerful, persistent,
energetic, and unencumbered by the ruins of the past, it
would realize republican ideals. But to see life breathed
into the ideals of socialism, one would have to turn to
Russia. "Let us leave the ancients to their old age, the

strong to their strength, and let us Slavs consecrate our efforts and our labors to the seed in our soil." [7]

Herzen's Slavophilism of the left and Aksakov's of the right demonstrate that even when (rhetorical excess notwithstanding) there was reason to think that the two nations shared common goals and aspirations, Russians were far from unanimous in the belief that America could or should be an object of admiration, a model, or a partner for them. There was never a single Russian view of America; different groups or individuals had diverse perceptions of the transatlantic republic, its society and institutions. It is quite untrue, therefore, to say, as an American journalist did in 1946, that before the Bolshevik Revolution, and to a surprising degree afterward, Russians had "almost universally . . . a conception of the United States as a manmade paradise and of Americans as muscular, upright, free and happy demigods.[8] From the writings of Russia's leading intellectuals and artists it is possible to arrive at the opposite conclusion.

Its most influential and famous thinkers, social critics, and writers, from the first Slavophiles in the early nineteenth century to the Marxists at the beginning of the twentieth, held and presented an image of the New World that was bleak, not very new, and, most important, lacking in hope. With one or two notable or partial exceptions, the luminaries of Russian thought and letters rendered a negative judgment of the United States, of its excesses of materialism and mass democracy, of its plutocracy and corruption, of its crassness and cruelty.

The power and persistence of America's defects in the minds of Russia's cultural and political elites across ideologies and generations are truly remarkable; the more so, since very few of them had first- or even second-hand knowledge of the United States. They came to America, whether in thought or person, with negative preconceptions. The hopes America had aroused and disappointed helped to account for this. The main reason, however, was a widely shared faith that Russian principles, whether communal, socialist, religious, or nativist, pointed the way to the future of man. The Russia of the mind was bound to be more beautiful, harmonious, and humane than the land across the sea. In any comparison between Russian utopia and American reality, America had to be, and still is, the loser. It had come very quickly to appear less a new beginning than the extension of an old and declining Europe.

If the North's fight against slavery, planters, and particularism had refurbished America's tarnished image for some—the radical critic Nikolai Chernyshevskii had greeted the Civil War as a revolution whose influence would spread to Europe—its aftermath confirmed and deepened older views and feelings. The period of American exceptionalism was over; the classical land of political liberty, the Populist philosopher Petr Lavrov wrote in 1876, had turned into the Republic of Humbug and the Empire of the Dollar, the home of an exploitative industrial capitalism that liberated slaves and women only to turn them into lackeys and proletarians. America's single-minded pursuit of wealth and its surrender of ideals when they conflicted with interests had become commonplaces for those who were not conservative or romantic nationalists.[9]

Dostoevsky's America was a country for weak, foolish, or desperate men, a place of soulless materialism and spiritual shallowness, of coarse manners and false promises of happiness and social justice. It was, in short, the quintessential West, the extension and enlargement of a world of selfishness and rootlessness, the place to which criminals might flee to save themselves but where there was no salvation, which could be gained only by pious labor on native soil, for and among one's own people. At best, as for Dmitrii Karamazov, America is a kind of Siberia where he will expiate his sins by exile and hardship and from which, if he does not perish from spiritual and physical want, he will return to Russia and the Russian

God. To a 1901 visitor from the United States, Tolstoi deplored that nation's preoccupation with material things, with "mills and railroads and the like," and he thought it sad that Russian statesmen were following "in the footsteps of yours in the matter of manufacturing and commercialism in general." As Dostoevsky had written thirty years before in his notes for *The Possessed*, "the world can live without America, without railroads, even without bread." [10]

What Vladimir Korolenko and Maksim Gorkii told their many readers about America was given weight by the fact that they were the only writers of prominence and stature who visited the United States before 1917. Korolenko spent two months there in 1893, and although he understood its lure for the dispossessed and downtrodden and had words of praise for its free institutions, he too saw it as a country lacking in joy, humanity, and justice. He noted unemployment, exploitation, corruption, and cruelty. The factories that produced the country's wealth and comforts inspired him with horror, especially those "factories of death" in Chicago's stockyards that proudly displayed how millions of animals were slaughtered in the most highly mechanized way. America's history, Korolenko concluded, was little more than a slaughterhouse; black slavery and the extermination of the Indians had left their mark on the national character. America might be all right for Americans; as for himself, he would rather live in Siberian Iakutia, where he had once been exiled. "Only here," he wrote from the United States, "do you feel and understand that our people, ignorant and enslaved, is nonetheless, by nature, the best of all peoples. That is not only a phrase and it is not Slavophilism. We lack liberty, but we are worthy of it." More worthy, it was implied, than those who had abused their freedoms. [11]

Even more influential were Gorkii's intemperate accounts of his American trip, for he became and remained after his death in 1936 a cultural hero of the Soviet

regime. Gorkii arrived in New York in April 1906 and
stayed for six months. He came to win sympathy and
raise funds for the revolutionary movement, and in particular for its Marxist wing. His distaste for American
ways and values was almost instantaneous, and it was
recorded in May and June in sketches and articles that
were published in Russia between September 1906 and
March 1907. His angry indictments of the "City of the
Yellow Devil" or "City of Mammon," of its millionaire
rulers (the "Kings of the Republic") and their faceless
slaves, have become standard texts. Although they added
little that was new to the chorus of denigration, there
was a special edge to Gorkii's strictures, for they included
workers, farmers, and immigrants—"Europe's rubbish,
its waste matter." A letter Gorkii wrote from the Adi-
rondacks is strikingly similar to Korolenko's rediscovery,
from afar, of the native virtues of Russia's simple people.
"We are far ahead of this free America for all our misfor-
tunes. This becomes especially apparent when you com-
pare the local farmer or workman with our peasants and
workers." [12] Such a sentimental declaration of Russian
superiority was strange for a proletarian writer to make.
Yet it was squarely in a tradition to which men from different parts of the political spectrum had contributed. In
that tradition, Russia's very backwardness gave assurance
of a future brighter than anything the new world, discovered to be neither very new nor brave, had achieved
or was likely to achieve.

"What idiots are all those Tverskois and other Russian
authors like him who write about America," Gorkii complained in his letter. It was, in fact, men like Tverskoi,
most of them liberal journalists or lesser literati, who per-
petuated the benign image of America that had been
shaped in 1776. Their names have little resonance—
Svinin, Lakier, Ogorodnikov, Tsimmerman, to list only
a few. Yet their many articles and books, recording personal experiences, were more accessible and interesting
to the general reader than the philosophical or artistic

productions of their illustrious compatriots. Without them, it is hard to account for the friendly fascination with America that was found among Russians of all classes. Nor is it possible to explain, without assuming that their reports found a positive response, why between 1900 and 1914 approximately 160,000 ethnic Russians emigrated to the United States, as many more Jews, Poles, and others had done before them. The vast majority of Great Russian immigrants were of peasant and worker origin. They felt, one traveler remarked with more than a trace of exaggeration, as if they were in paradise, whereas newcomers of the intelligentsia were bitterly disappointed.[18]

The rights and institutions that so many of the intelligentsia thought inadequate to the attainment of social justice and equality, and nationalists of various stripes destructive of inner freedom and faith, were not without Russian admirers. Their initial discovery of America had been a political one, and the conquest of national and individual liberty in the American Revolution had made heroes of its leaders, whose names were known and toasted in remote Siberia by officials of the Empress Catherine. Nicholas Novikov, moral and social reformer, saw the foundation of the new republic as a moral as well as a political act and Benjamin Franklin and John Adams as kindred spirits in the fight against the vices of courts and aristocracies. "Vashington" was the greatest of liberators and patriots, and the nation he had created a refuge for the liberty that luxury and depravity had driven from Europe.

For Alexander Radishchev, Russia's first radical and abolitionist, the American Revolution was a popular rising against the abuses of arbitrary government and part of the universal battle for the freedom and dignity of all men. Not even slavery could extinguish for Radishchev the achievement of political and civil liberty, and few Russians after him spoke of America with such passion. For the insurgent officers who rose against the autocracy

in December 1825, the United States furnished the model
of a revolution that had avoided despotism and terror and
of a constitutional federation in which the rights of men
were secure and the powers of government restrained.
America proved that a state need not be cruel to be
strong or rulers tyrannical to be obeyed.[14]

The first Russian visitor to publish accounts of the
young republic, the diplomat Pavel Svinin, was impressed
by its manufactures, inventions, and bold commercial en-
terprises, by its libraries, learned societies, and public
schools. Education and virtue bestowed the right to a
share in making the nation's laws which, in spite of
shoddy electioneering and party feuds, were wise and just,
proving the people worthy of their liberties. The empire's
minister to Washington, after a stay of more than ten
years (1809–1822), also marveled at the spectacular
progress that a nation free of external threats, a standing
army, and religious persecution had made under a government that gave a wide latitude to talents and energies.
All was in motion, he wrote, and rapidly advancing toward a better order of things.[15]

That was the view also that Alexander Lakier conveyed
in the book that told of his travels in 1857. Freedom was
America's energizing and animating principle, and it was
certain to exert its influence over Europe, not by force of
arms, not by fire and sword, but by the power of inven-
tion, by commerce and industry, whose influence would
be more lasting than conquests. It was their freedoms,
another traveler, P. I. Ogorodnikov, agreed a decade later,
that had made the Americans daring and successful, and
their schools were the "front and bulwark" of those freedoms. Dostoevsky was as distressed by Ogorodnikov's
American diaries as Gorkii would be angered by Tverskoi's, for they considered materialism the condition of
American liberty, the guarantee not only of comfort but
also of individual independence and dignity, a safeguard
against extremes of misery and luxury. America, Ogorodnikov conceded, had not made all her people virtuous

or happy. But she had put virtue and happiness within the reach of all, without distinction of class or caste. The blessings of liberty were not a utopian dream but the reality of America.[16]

Few Russians knew that reality better than P. A. Tverskoi, and none wrote of it in such knowledgeable and concrete detail. A political refugee, he had made his way to Florida in 1881 to take up farming, at which he failed, and with the last of his capital became partner in a lumber mill. Soon he was launched on a successful career in business, settled in California, and, except for two extended trips to Russia, remained there until his death in 1919. Success and well being undoubtedly deepened his attachment to his adopted country. Yet neither in his book of 1895[17] nor in his subsequent writings did Tverskoi conceal that he was troubled by much of what was happening in America's domestic and foreign affairs.

He described for his countrymen the wide spread of literacy, political participation, and awareness; the general competence, confidence, and civic pride; advanced manufacturing processes and business practices; the high skills and productivity of workmen and their successful struggle for decent wages and hours; high standards of commercial honesty; excellent communications; the easy availability of credit and information and of the opportunity this gave to men of small means and large visions. He wrote of the power and crimes of the monopolists and trusts, of the fever of speculation that seized every American, of sharp business dealings and fierce competition, of strikes, unemployment, and lockouts, of political chicanery and corruption. During and after the Spanish-American War and the growth of chauvinistic sentiment fanned by the yellow press, he returned repeatedly and worriedly to the subject of imperialism and the threat it posed to the nation's good name, good sense, and Constitution. He was equally troubled by the machinations of the napoleons of industry and finance and in 1902 voiced the fear that they might enslave the country and produce an economic revolution of unpredictable consequences.

Tverskoi's pessimism did not last. Although he continued to see dangers in a variety of quarters, he also noted tendencies to check these. The widespread agitation for political and social reform, the peace and labor movements, gave hope that arbitration and conciliation would take the place of conflict at home and abroad. Tverskoi reaffirmed his belief in the soundness of the American system in 1910: "The Union is facing difficult times, a sharp and extraordinarily important conflict from which there will emerge a healthier, more sensible political order free of the intrigues of unprincipled politicians." [18]

When in April 1917, a month after the fall of the Romanovs, the United States became Russia's ally in the war against Germany, both countries rediscovered the affinities they had proclaimed in 1886. Woodrow Wilson declared that Russia had always been democratic at heart and that her people, after shaking off an alien autocracy, had become a worthy partner in the fight for freedom in the world. The head of the Provisional Government announced that Russians, having in one jump reached America's freedom, could now embark on the task of overtaking her in education, material progress, culture, and respect for order. At army headquarters, General Brusilov told an American delegation: "Here, as across the ocean, you will find the same banner bearing the same great device—liberty, civil, social, political, and national." Foreign Minister Miliukov, a leader of the Constitutional Democratic Party, assured the American ambassador that the ideals represented by his government were "the same as underlie the existence of your own nation." [19]

The liberals' perception of America, like liberalism itself, did not prevail. Neither had made a permanent conquest of the Russian mind. The Provisional Government had soon to yield to the powerful yearning of the masses for peace and equality. In March 1918, the new Soviet government withdrew from a war whose aims it considered imperialistic rather than democratic, putting an end to the short-lived community of ideals and interests. The America of "multimillionaires and capitalist sharks" (Lenin), a participant in Allied intervention against Bolshevism, emerged as its greatest adversary. Even so, some Bolsheviks conceded, as did Lenin in August 1918, that the democratic republic of the United States—where "you have feudal servitude for millions of workers and unrelieved destitution"—was also the freest and most civilized country in the world. The memories of 1776, a truly great and liberating revolution, and of the Civil War were still alive, and Lenin's invoking them made possible their use when his successors wished or needed to recall what the two countries had in common.[20]

Both before and after the Bolshevik Revolution in October 1917, what Russians knew best and most generally liked or envied about the United States was the economic and technical miracle that had transformed a rude nation—much like their own in many respects—into a mighty and prosperous power. The Americans' inventiveness, their genius in practical and technical matters, had been proverbial ever since Franklin and Fulton came to Russian notice. McCormick reapers and Baldwin locomotives, the Morse telegraph and the Singer sewing machines, the bridges of Roebling and the Patent Office at Washington provided evidence of the Americans' ingenuity and the productivity of their fields and factories. By the turn of the century, urban Russia also knew Edison's phonograph, Bell's telephone, Otis's elevators, Kodak's cameras, and Remington's typewriters. Like the steamboat for Svinin in 1814 and other mechanical marvels for those who followed him, they stood as symbols of daring and progress, of an openness to innovation and experimentation that was unique to the new world; they

also bore the promise of lifting from mankind the burdens
of toil and the curse of scarcity, of dignifying the labor
of all and rewarding it fairly.

In 1899, long before it became a rallying cry for Stalin's
Five-Year Plans, the famous chemist Dmitrii Mendeleev
posited "catching up with America" as a national goal.
And so often did he point to America as an example that
he felt on one occasion constrained to explain that he
did not think her an ideal country in every respect. Russians sought wealth and power not as ends in themselves,
as the Americans did, but as the means to a richer unfolding of the national spirit. Another "troubadour of
industrialism," as the economist Ivan Ozerov referred to
himself, time and again called between 1900 and 1915
in his copious professional and popular writings for an
"injection of Americanism." Stripped of its excesses, it
would enable Russians to overcome backwardness and
sloth, bureaucratic arbitrariness and immobilism, the excessive reliance of business on the state and the excess of
drinking and holidays, low literacy and discipline on the
part of labor. For Ozerov, as for Mendeleev and other
pragmatic Americanists, America and what it stood for—
boldness, modernity, and legal protection given to individuals and their efforts—were the slogan and banner that
would propel sluggish Russia forward on the road America had already traveled. Young Russians, in particular,
Ozerov hoped, learning in and about the United States,
would furnish the impetus and energy needed to overcome the traditionalism, inertia, and prejudices of an
older generation and an old regime.[21]

II

The young generation of revolutionaries that replaced
the old regime wanted to remake not only Russia but the
world in an image for which no model existed anywhere.
That Russia's Marxist leaders and mentors would look
upon the United States with hostility was a certainty.

Emerging from the First World War as the most powerful country of the capitalist world, it was bound to be
seen as the chief obstacle to world revolution. And ideo-
logically, the very successes and appeals of America's
democracy and economy constituted a challenge that
could not be ignored. Lenin never doubted that the
bourgeoisie in the New World was as exploitative as in
the old, and even more so. Because America was the
youngest and most progressive capitalist nation, it had
also developed the most unbridled and advanced forms
of wage slavery, with the highest degree of concentration
in industry, agriculture, and finance. The result was "ap-
palling unemployment and poverty, a wanton waste of
human labor side by side with the unprecedented luxury
of the multimillionaires" who were the nation's real rulers
and kept the masses in subjection and servitude. But the
American proletariat was awakening, no longer willing to
be fobbed off by the reformist promises of bourgeois politicians. Even before the sharpening of class conflict
brought by the war, Lenin saw an increase in the number
of socialist votes as a clear sign of "the kind of revolution
that is approaching in America." After the war he pre-
dicted that American workers will "be with us for civil
war against the bourgeoisie." In 1919, Grigorii Zinoviev,
head of the Comintern, greeted the newly formed American Communist Party as "the first swallow which fore-
tells the coming of a world-wide Communist spring." [22]

Vladimir Maiakovskii, futurist poet and bard of the
revolution, prophesied in the same year that its irresistible
march would take it across the Atlantic where it would
plant the red flag on the buildings of New York and
rouse the miners of California. In a 1920 poem, "150
000 000," the giant peasant Ivan wades across the sea to
do battle in Chicago, the quintessential American city,
with Woodrow Wilson, the archetypical American capitalist. In his grossness and gluttony, Wilson is very much
like the kings of the republic cartooned by Gorkii. He
eats from early morning until late at night—meat, butter,

and a hundred bottles of cream. He is waited upon by Lincolns, Whitmans, Edisons, and the "king of poets," Longfellow. His top hat is as tall as a tower, and his trousers are made of American poetry. With a twiddle of his thumbs, he can cause workers to be fired from their factories or a golden rain to fall on the mansions of the rich.

Maiakovskii did not see America until 1925. He had gone, he explained, to discover with his own eyes, and at its highest level of development, the industrial American-ism he and other futurists had preached. Lonely, ignorant of any Western language, and dispirited by the summer heat, he found the cities dirty and unlovely, the people absorbed in the chase and worship of the dollar from morning to night, from childhood to old age, in their public as well as in their most private relationships. They were but a "union of foreigners for exploitation, specula-tion, and trade." The futurism of naked technology, its most impressive emblem being the Brooklyn Bridge—"That's quite a creation!"—had proved itself. It had not, however, revolutionized a "paralyzed, obese, and ancient psyche" and could not do so by itself. In its spiritual poverty and political backwardness America belonged to a past that Russians were putting behind them. Maiakov-skii felt he had rushed forward seven thousand versts in space only to move backward seven years in time, and he told an interviewer that there was more energy, the collective energy of a liberated people, in the torn-up streets and among the broken-down houses of Moscow than in the richest and busiest quarters of New York.[23]

The terms and tones of Maiakovskii's anti-American-ism—emotional and ideological, old and new—predomi-nated in the literature and propaganda of the following years. The Great Depression in particular seemed to prove that the stronghold of capitalism was not immune to decay and strengthened expectations of a final, revo-lutionary, and not-too-distant crisis. Yet this was far from all that Soviet citizens or their leaders knew about the rival republic in the 1920s and 1930s. The latter were not nearly so dismissive of its strength and values as they sounded, while the former, although constantly reminded of desperate workers and oppressed Negroes, thought of America as a land of plenty and splendor which they flocked to see in the Hollywood films decried by their betters but allowed as a relief from a drab reality.[24]

By its exhortations to catch up with and overtake America, the regime validated the popular image and admitted that the abstractions of Marxist theory were not enough to enlist the masses in the superhuman effort of forced-draft industrialization. Russia, a Soviet educator said shortly after the revolution, was to be a second America, but without capitalism. They want Russia to be like America, Theodore Dreiser sadly noted after his 1927 visit, "its cities like Chicago and Detroit, its leaders and geniuses like Ford and Rockefeller, Edison and Gary." Maurice Hindus, a Russian-born American writer, was asked by a villager in 1930 whether there were collective farms in America. No? Well, then perhaps they were not a good thing, because if they were, America would surely have them, as she had cars and steam-heated houses, oranges and lemons in profusion.[25]

Although diplomatic relations were not established until 1933 and anxious guardians of socialist doctrine and culture warned that the evils of capitalism tainted all its products, the Soviet government and people did not turn their backs on the United States. "Ours is the only important government which refuses to grant Russia political recognition," an American journalist wrote, "and yet it is our country that Russia emulates and admires." Nowhere else, Hindus discovered, was it so widely idolized. America stood for competence, responsibility, punctuality, accuracy, and diligence, for work carried on steadily and with an economy of materials and effort, with daring inventiveness and a readiness to depart from routine. America represented youth and invincibility, the triumph of the machine and mass production, the possibility of ending scarcity and inequality. American efficiency, Stalin hymned in 1924, was an indomitable force that neither knew nor recognized obstacles and did not rest until a task was finished. "Without it, serious constructive work is impossible . . . The combination of Russian revolutionary sweep and American efficiency is the essence of Leninism in party and state work." [26]

About 3,000 American engineers worked in the Soviet Union in the early thirties, and of 125 technical-aid agreements, by far the largest number was concluded with American firms in almost every branch of production. This massive transfer of American production techniques and the assistance of American specialists represented the injection of Americanism Ozerov had advocated. The Americans had helped a great deal, Stalin acknowledged in 1933, "helped us better and more boldly than the others," and during World War II he was quoted as saying that American technology had been used in two-thirds of the new plants built in the U.S.S.R. [27]

The United States was not the only or even primary source of men, methods, and machines during the Five-Year Plans; more German than American specialists, for example, were recruited. But it was the favored one. Close economic relations with America, Commissar of Trade Mikoyan declared in 1930, are the most attractive to us because of its advanced technology, the scale of its economy, and because it is the leader in mass production and standardization. [28] America was also the most palatable partner for other reasons. Despite ritualistic denunciations and forecasts of its imminent doom, there was more good will and feeling for America, its people and institutions, than for England or Germany. The American connection was free of ancient hostilities and injured sensibilities; real or imagined similarities of climate, size, national character, or temperament made the ingenious, energetic, open Yankee, who lacked a feudal past, a more acceptable model or helper than the stiff, class-conscious Englishman or the deliberate and overbearing German.

The war scare created by the regime in 1927 concentrated on Britain as the chief imperialist power, and in the show trials of foreign engineers staged between 1928 and 1933 no Americans were indicted for "wrecking." Only one of the American specialists who appeared in the novels and plays of "socialist construction" is unmasked as a saboteur, and he is eventually discovered to be British. The American engineer of fiction may be limited in his political understanding, even hostile to the Soviet experiment and interested in it only to make money, but more often than not he is a sympathetic figure who performs his work conscientiously, and in his democratic manners, his willingness to get his hands and boots dirty, he sets a good example for his hosts. In the late 1930s, the years of the Great Purges, he disappears from Russian life and literature, an increasingly shrill and paranoid nationalism that sees enemies everywhere, at home and abroad, displaces Americanism.[29]

America itself remained an object of intense if unsatisfied curiosity, and the account that two well-known humorists, Ilf and Petrov, published of their travels in 1936 became the most widely read Soviet book about the United States. It was acceptable because it contained all the required stereotypes about the darker sides of American life and popular because its authors had a light touch, were clearly charmed by much of what they found, and, unlike Maiakovskii and Gorki, enjoyed their stay and the coast-to-coast auto trip they took in the company of a genial American couple. They saw more than the great cities, with their extremes of wealth and poverty, the dehumanizing assembly lines of Ford, vulgar advertising, and infantile films. They also discovered a land of one- or two-storied houses in small towns where most Americans lived, great natural beauty, and people who were energetic, efficient, boundlessly hospitable, and true to their word. For all its riches, comforts, and spurious freedoms, America, of course, was dangerously ill and unhappy. Yet the spirit of democracy was strong in everyday life and worthy of imitation, for it could "help a lot in work, deliver a blow to bureaucratism, and enhance human dignity." [30]

One-Storied America was a model of objectivity compared with the scurrilous and vicious distortions Soviet presses poured forth during the next two decades. The caricatures created by gifted writers such as Ilya Ehrenburg, as well as by anonymous hacks, were hardly affected by the wartime coalition with the West. Only rarely did Soviet leaders find it opportune to mention, as Stalin did in November 1941, the "elementary democratic liberties" the Allied peoples enjoyed as those of the Fascist states did not. Grudgingly, and only in the darkest days of the war, when Russian morale needed boosting, did they publicly mention the productive prowess, the military might, and the aid of the United States. A *Pravda* review of the military and political events of 1944 did not once mention England or America. A 1942 secondary-school text in modern history was revised in 1944 to eliminate a paragraph about the tradition of friendship between the Russian and American peoples. Press discussions of domestic affairs in the United States dealt almost exclusively with the growth of pro-Soviet sympathies among "progressive" elements and their clamor for a second front.[31]

Fears that too close an embrace of the American ally would lead the population to expect an ideological softening and a relaxation of controls were justified; measures to dampen such hopes were only partially successful. There was an American air base in the Ukraine and other evidence of the United States in the form of trucks, jeeps, boots, and tins of Spam throughout the army and the country. Several days after the victory over Germany, an enormous spontaneous demonstration of friendship took place before the American embassy. George Kennan, who addressed the crowd, recalled that it was the only place in Moscow where a display of such warmth and size took place. "It is not hard to imagine what mortification this must have brought to both party and police." [32]

Mortification and fear led the Soviet leaders to unprecedented exertions to isolate and insulate their people from contamination by the bourgeois world and to present it in the most dismal colors: aggressive and imperialistic abroad, repressive and corrupt at home, destined to perish from its inherent contradictions, yet powerful and desperate enough to pose a mortal threat to the "camp of socialism." The United States, with its monopoly of the atom bomb, emerged as the enemy incarnate, no longer a mere ideological antagonist or the outstanding example of a capitalism at once chaotic and ruthlessly efficient, but the actual leader and inspirer, financier and armorer of a campaign to deny to the Soviet Union the fruits of victory and to reverse history's march toward socialism. Symbols of evil were gradually transferred from Nazi Germany to reactionary America. In July 1945 the journal *Bolshevik* accused America's capitalists of having assisted Hitler in his rise to power, and in January 1948, the head of the Party's propaganda department charged that the "American imperialists are clearly seeking to take the place of Fascist Germany and Japan ..." [33]

By then, the "anti-cosmopolitan" campaign associated with Andrei Zhdanov was fully launched and its chief target identified. It touched every sphere of life and was intolerant of the slightest deviation. The prominent economist Evgenii Varga was forced to recant the heresy that America might be able to stave off the general crisis of capitalism for a time and achieve a degree of economic stability through planning, and that it would not enter lightly into armed conflict. Other Vargists were accused of groveling before the technical-economic might of the United States, and Russians were claimed to have invented the light bulb and the airplane before Edison and the Wrights. Public use of the word *jazz* was forbidden, the State Jazz Orchestra was renamed the State Variety

Orchestra, and every saxophonist in Moscow was ordered to turn in his instrument. Theaters and movie houses showed dozens of anti-American films and plays with such titles as *The Mad Haberdasher* and *Conspiracy of the Doomed*. They drew far smaller audiences than the Hollywood productions that had been captured in Germany and given Russian subtitles. Deanna Durbin, Shirley Temple, and Tarzan, along with the Communist Party of the United States, were almost the only exceptions to the general embargo. Others were "progressive" writers whose "American Tales" fell into the hands of an inmate in Solzhenitsyn's *First Circle*. "Khorobrov could not verify these stories by comparing them with life, but the selection was surprising. In every story there was some obligatory abomination about America. Venomously assembled, they made up such a nightmarish picture that one could only be amazed that the Americans had not yet fled their country or hanged themselves." [34]

After Stalin's death in 1953 it became possible for his successors to admit more realistic and less monochromatic pictures of the outside world; indeed, it became necessary to overcome the rigidities and stagnation that were the legacy of his rule. The "thaw" was not a radical reversal but a controlled correction of course that was marked by hesitancies, partial retreats, and the resistance of Stalinist diehards.

The rediscovery of America began with the arcane debates of scholars, some of whom, including Varga, maintained that orthodox simplicities were inadequate to an understanding of a system that consisted of more than a state dominated by a few monopolists and a mass of workers whom that state, at the monopolists' bidding, oppressed. The bourgeois state, they held, was not entirely or always subordinate to its capitalist masters who were themselves divided by economic, regional, even personal differences and conflicts. The greatest importance of such a finding—that there were moderate and reasonable men as well as blind reactionaries and anti-Communist crusaders among America's leaders—lay, of course, in the field of foreign policy, where it allowed for an accommodation that promised greater benefits than continual and costly confrontation. Nikita Khrushchev placed his stamp of approval on this line of argument when he distinguished, at the Twentieth Party Congress in 1956, between the "more farsighted representatives of the imperialist ruling circles" and "the more rabid proponents of the 'position of strength' policy." [35]

Détente with the United States also held out the prospect of closing, through a reduction in arms expenditures and the exchange of information and specialists, the gap in science and technology that Stalinist isolationism had widened. That the Soviet Union had been left behind in the second industrial revolution was obvious to senior scientists and economists who were aware of the great strides America had made with the help of superior technology, management techniques, and the wide application of science to production. The public continued to be told that the United States faced economic decline and crisis and that the Soviet Union was training more and better specialists. The launching of Sputnik lent substance to that claim; it did not diminish Soviet interest in an exchange agreement and may have increased American readiness to sign one in January 1958. Later that year, Khrushchev proposed to President Eisenhower an increase in trade that would include industrial equipment. Soviet commentators on that occasion recalled the mutually beneficial experiences of the twenties and thirties. They and their readers also may have been reminded of the slogans used then by their revival in 1959: within a decade per capita production in the U.S.S.R. would reach American levels; by 1975 they would be overtaken in volume, Premier Kosygin told the Supreme Soviet in 1971. "America," Khrushchev wrote in the memoirs he composed after his forced retirement in 1964, "occupied a special position in our thinking and our views of the world." [36]

The leaders who followed him insisted that the economic tasks and problems they faced could be solved
without foreign help. Yet their expansion of détente in
the 1970s was motivated to a significant degree by the
wish to see these problems eased and their solution
speeded through an infusion of American technology.
The economy of the United States, a leading foreign-
affairs analyst stated in the first issue of the journal SShA
(USA), more than that of any other capitalist country,
stimulates scientific and technical progress. The trade
and scientific-technical agreements signed during and
after the visits Secretary General Brezhnev and President
Nixon exchanged in 1972 and 1973 exceeded all previous
ones in number and scope. But the level of cultural ex-
changes remained moderate for several years. After the
Moscow summit meeting, Brezhnev warned, as Khrushchev had done, that peaceful coexistence implied no
weakening of the ideological struggle that would intensify
and become a still-sharper form of the antagonism between the two systems.[37]

The danger that détente might be taken as a warrant
for more open contacts between peoples, cultures, and
ideologies was real. The riotous receptions given the
Benny Goodman tour in 1962 confirmed one function-
ary's fears that "we are losing the youth" and led Khrushchev to declare that jazz made him feel as if he had gas
on the stomach. His condemnation of "peaceful coexistence in the field of ideology as treason to Marxism-
Leninism" was part of a general indictment of modern-
ism in art, architecture, and music, which he delivered to
a large Kremlin audience in March 1963 and linked with
the capitalist threat.[38] Among his special targets, besides
jazz, were the poets Evgenii Evtushenko and Andrei
Voznesenskii and the novelist Viktor Nekrasov. They
had incurred official displeasure because of the "political
immaturity" in their writings about America in their conduct abroad. Nekrasov was the chief culprit. He was attacked again in June before the Central Committee of

the Communist Party whose First Secretary urged Nekrasov's expulsion from the Party and criticized his book
On Both Sides of the Ocean.

A certain tourist goes to America and sees one side of it,
which he is earnestly shown by people assigned for the purpose, and, having returned home, he thinks: "Well, now,
that's what America is like." But such an individual's personal misapprehensions are a minor difficulty. It is much worse
if he begins to propagandize his mistaken impressions and
views, the concepts foisted upon him by a hostile ideology, to
propagandize them everywhere as the only true concept.[39]

Khrushchev would have preferred that Gorkii and Ilf
and Petrov serve as his countrymen's guides to America,
as they had done for him in 1959.[40] But neither America
nor Nekrasov's falling victim to America's blandishments
was the real issue. He had, it is true, expressed enthusiasm
for the grandeur and beauty of cities, skyscrapers, and
bridges; delight in modern art and architecture; tolerance
for Elvis Presley and a liking for Coca Cola; gratitude for
food he had received as a child from the American Relief Association in 1922 and for the tanks, planes, trucks,
and canned pork supplied in World War II. He had also
refused to repeat what had been said so often about slums
and urban blight, the misery of the unemployed, and the
plight of the blacks. "We saw all of this and it exists.
But is it really worth while going to a foreign country if
this is all that interests you?" [41]

Superficiality and an attitude of compromise, one critic
complained, had caused Nekrasov to ignore what even
the reactionary American press did not conceal: the cry-
ing social contradictions, the unchecked reign of militarism, the McCarthyist hysteria. His gravest sin was
pointed out in *Izvestiia*. Striving for balance in his description of the factual aspects of American life, he had
fallen into the far more serious error of applying the
fifty-fifty rule when comparing the two worlds, the two
ideologies.[42] And so he had, subtly yet unmistakably. If

the American authorities did not allow his group of tourists to go everywhere, neither did its leader wish them to do so on their own. Television was not the scourge of America alone; at home it drove viewers into the depths of boredom with its endless and interchangeable interview and amateur shows. Surrealism was a much more complex phenomenon than admitted by the *Great Soviet Encyclopedia*. "But some of our painters seem to be running just as hard to . . . a carefully flattened, exultingly saccharine kind of anti-reality." A true work of art is living water. "And we have been getting dead water for so long now." Yes, America was inundated by a dark stream of police and detective novels, but its many bookstores also contained a great many good, interesting, and serious (if expensive) books. At home, Kafka was unknown and unpublished.[43]

Nekrasov was made to revise his book, and no other like it has appeared in the Soviet Union, which he left in 1974. But despite fluctuations in the domestic political climate (Nekrasov was finally expelled from the Party in 1972) and a distinct chill in relations with America that began in the late seventies, there has been no return to the darkest days of Stalinist winter, which is not to say that distortion has given way to fairness and rejection to acceptance in the treatment of American society and culture; only that it became more sophisticated and diverse, that relatively sober works of scholarship were produced along with tracts of propaganda and reportage containing a mixture of the two.

The government's need for accurate information contributed to greater realism and diversity with the establishment of the Moscow Institute of the USA and Canada in 1967 and of centers of American studies at several universities to train a larger cadre of Americanists than the country had ever possessed. An explosive growth in the number of scholarly studies on many aspects of American society and history—many of them enriched by first-hand knowledge—was exceeded by an even greater output of popular and semipopular works. Their large editions, television programs, and the still more numerous articles in the press testify to a lasting curiosity about life in the United States as well as to official concern that it should be presented in a politically correct yet palatable way. A too heavy-handed approach, it was realized, would be counterproductive with audiences that had grown distrustful of crass distortions, inured to simple slogans, and that included individuals who have access—via foreign broadcasts and thousands of Western and Soviet travelers —to alternative sources of information. Deep-seated cultural misunderstandings and incomprehensions remain, as do ideological boundaries that cannot be crossed and verities that cannot be questioned—such as the irremediable sicknesses and iniquities of American capitalism. The latter, elaborated on in familiar as well as novel ways, appear most often in the mass media and in publications designed for those entrusted with the guidance and instruction of their fellow citizens.

A ten-year sampling, covering the years 1970–1980, reveals what Russians were most likely to hear and read about:[44] America's lack or loss of ideals; loneliness in the midst of crowds and manufactured cheer; a stifling atmosphere of individualism and cynicism that strengthens the dictatorship of the bourgeoisie; a people kept in ignorance by its schools and sensationalist press; monotonous skyscrapers and dangerous superhighways, at once irrational and inhuman; hundreds of thousands fleeing "paradise" and millions more (one out of eight) wishing to emigrate; organized and random violence that kills progressive leaders, makes parks and subways unsafe for ordinary people, and turns New York into a jungle during a power failure; cultural philistinism and vulgarity; "narcomania" and pornography and the profits they bring to a few; the chronic crisis in health care and the deeper crisis in the nation's spirit revealed by the Jonestown massacre. "America is a society without a future," *Pravda* declared on January 15 of the bicentennial year, while a television commentator saw in the speed limit imposed to conserve gasoline a symbol of the country's slowing down, a loss of dynamism and confidence.

These lurid tableaus of degeneration overshadowed and outnumbered, but did not supplant, the thrice-told and therefore less arresting tales of racism, repression, and economic decline: Puerto Ricans treated like half-beggared stepsons of rich America; Negro children dying of hunger in Mississippi; downtrodden illiterate Indians on reservations; cruel reprisals against Black Panthers in Chicago and outrages against black schoolchildren in Boston; the bullets of Klansmen and the brass knuckles of neo-Nazis; a system of police surveillance that turns 1984 into a report of life under capitalism; the power of America's Fortune 500 corporations and "uncrowned kings"— Morgans, Rockefellers, and Duponts, Fords, Gettys, and Hunts—whose interests are served by both political parties and who grow richer as the poor grow poorer; the general crisis of capitalism that manifests itself in strikes, bank failures, and deficits, in skyrocketing inflation and unemployment and cannot be cured by demagogic programs of relief.

"The crisis in the United States is growing steadily worse," a *Pravda* commentator wrote on October 14, 1974, at the height of détente. Why then was it thought possible or desirable to coexist, trade, even collaborate with a country so riddled with strife, enfeebled by calamities, and likely to seek a way out of its difficulties in aggression? For the advocates of détente the answer lay in the overriding necessity to avoid a nuclear catastrophe. In their debates with hard-liners and traditionalists they were supported by realists who had been arguing for some time that the monopolies and the military-industrial complex did not hold undisputed sway, that they were challenged by forces—in industry and in Congress, in the bureaucracy and the intellectual community—more influential than the shadowy proletariat and the Communist Party. The realists asked for concrete analyses of the concrete phenomena of American life and politics, and their most prominent spokesman, Georgii Arbatov, head of the USA Institute, took the lead in providing these to the leadership and the country.

In 1970 he noted that objective conditions made it possible for many democratic demands to be implemented without waiting for fundamental social and political transformations; in 1973 that many representatives of the ruling class had come to see the necessity and advantages of reducing foreign involvements and seeking an accommodation with the Soviet Union; in 1976 that two thirds of the public, 80 percent of the Congress, and 92 percent of the heads of the biggest corporations favored an increase in cooperation. These changes, Arbatov warned, were not irreversible—in 1980 he saw America returning to the "old cold war rut"—because of the class nature of American society, intrinsic capitalist hostility to socialism, and the inveterate opposition of reactionaries to the new realism.[45]

None of Arbatov's colleagues in the field of American studies lost sight of these central tenets of Marxism-Leninism, and all continue to be guided by them. But some felt encouraged by the new political realism in their own country to go beyond the labels that had for so long served in the place of analysis, to recover the more attractive features of the American past and admit greater complexity in examinations of the present.

On the shelves of bookstores and periodicals kiosks, standard denunciations of the malefactors of great wealth were joined by biographies of the imperialist president, Theodore Roosevelt, who had also denounced and fought them, of Washington, Franklin, Jefferson, and Lincoln. Franklin D. Roosevelt emerged as more than a manipulator who had staved off capitalism's collapse with half-hearted reforms—a man with a keen sense of the new who has "remained in the memory of humanity as an ardent advocate of international cooperation." [46] Studies of different trends and elements in the Republican Party and the social structure could be found side by side with pamphlets about the CIA and the Pentagon. The American Revolution, usually dismissed as merely a war for national independence and the supremacy of the native bourgeoisie, regained in some measure the liberating and revolutionary character Lenin had ascribed to it and its standing as a major battle against tyranny and for democracy. Equally great significance was attributed to the Civil War, the second American revolution, for testifying to the strength and uniqueness of the democratic and progressive tradition in American thought that stretched from Franklin, Jefferson, and Paine—a selection of their writings was published in 1977—to the abolitionist, agrarian, and workers' movements in the nineteenth century and inspired blacks and youth in the twentieth.

Americans were also found to possess, since the Spanish-American War, a tradition of "democratic isolationism and pacifism" that resurfaced at the time of American intervention against the young Soviet republic and helped to prepare the ground for its recognition in 1933.[47] Instances of cooperation, friendship, and mutual interest were recalled, from Russia's Declaration of Armed Neutrality during the War of Independence against Great Britain to the Grand Alliance of World War II against Germany; from the 1832 Treaty of Commerce and Navigation to 1932 when the U.S.S.R. took 40 percent of America's industrial exports; from Benjamin Franklin's election to the Imperial Academy of Sciences in 1789 to the meeting in space of Aleksei Leonov and Thomas Stafford in 1975; from the popularity of Cooper, Poe, and Hawthorne in nineteenth-century Russia to the warm reception given in the 1930s to the works of Soviet writers, composers, and film makers in the United States.

The work of fifty modern American poets was anthologized in 1976 and showed, Evtushenko wrote in *Pravda*, that they had withstood the standardized current of mass culture, commercialism, and cheap advertisements for the so-called American way of life. A diet once restricted largely to Mark Twain, Jack London, Theodore Dreiser, and Sinclair Lewis was enriched in the sixties and seventies by translations of Herman Melville and Henry James, John Cheever and William Faulkner, F. Scott Fitzgerald and J. D. Salinger, William Styron and Thomas Wolfe. Washington's Arena Stage, the Joffrey Ballet, recitalists, and orchestras demonstrated to Soviet audiences that America was not, after all, a cultural desert. The new tolerance extended even to a few Hollywood movies as well as to jazz and rock groups that visited the Soviet Union between 1975 and 1980.[48]

The limits and selectivity of tolerance are manifest, as is its sensitivity to changes in the international climate. Neither American rock musicians nor recordings have been welcome in the recent past, and the illicit trade in the latter has caused Radio Moscow to ask: "Have we really nothing with which to counter this whole dirty wave?" Not only does important work by important American writers remain untranslated (Robert Penn Warren, John Updike, Henry Miller, William Burroughs, Ezra Pound, Saul Bellow), it is also unavailable in the original, except to trusted scholars. Translators (of Studs Terkel, Truman Capote, Joseph Heller, and James Jones) have revised or shortened the originals to the point of deliberate and gross distortion. Senator Fulbright may have been acclaimed as a voice of sanity speaking for all Americans, but the Russian version of his *Arrogance of Power* (1967) more than once departs in language and spirit from the original, a fact of which neither author nor readers were informed. A facsimile edition of *Science*, distributed under an agreement with its publisher, the American Association for the Advancement of Science, has been heavily censored for years.[49]

It is certain that in the foreseeable future neither scientists nor ordinary Soviet citizens will be able to form their own unguided opinions about the outside world. Indeed, invidious comparison and a mirror that enlarges America's real problems may become more necessary as

domestic difficulties—from the loss of economic dynamism to cultural pessimism—multiply.

Beyond that, no confident conclusion can be drawn
or safe prediction made. For there are signs of division,
and perhaps confusion, in the official mind over how to
interpret the mass of information that is now available
on American society and politics and how to deal with
recent changes in the latter. In such a situation, the
temptation is great to fall back on the dogmatic cer-
tainties of an earlier day. In October 1983, for example,
the director of the Institute of World Economics and
International Relations took issue with "some politicians
and public figures [who] with a certain complacency are
inclined to believe that what is occurring in U.S. international policy today is a chance moment in history, an
irrational moment, which they attribute to Reagan's personal qualities." Far from a temporary aberration, the administration's militarism and chauvinism were of the
essence in American imperialism, a logical continuation
of what had been in preparation for many years and the
president the candidate of big business and the military-
industrial complex.[50]

Only a month later, the political commentator of
Izvestiia, A. Bovin, sounded a more hopeful note when
he recalled that Franklin Roosevelt's intelligence and
sense of history had facilitated the establishment of diplomatic ties with the U.S.S.R. fifty years earlier. Bovin
attributed the ups and downs in attitudes toward the
Soviet Union to changes in the White House, as well as
to clashes within the ruling circles of America, and looked
forward, sooner or later, to their realignment and an
improved relationship. In the Democratic draft platform
of March 1984 he detected elements of common sense
and realism that could lead to radical changes in foreign
policy. The fortieth anniversary of D-Day also gave rise
to conflicting reflections—that the Western powers had
postponed the second front in order to weaken the Soviet
army and that the wartime alliance, for all its short-

comings and frictions, had proved that states with different social systems could coexist and cooperate.[51]

The public mind and feelings are equally divided. Emigrés and foreigners who work or travel in the Soviet Union report that America evokes a wide range of responses—awe and admiration, critical respect, fear, and revulsion. To many who are deprived of intellectual or artistic freedom, who are threatened in their religious or national identity and suffer discrimination because of it, America is still a refuge offering liberty and equality, opportunities as well as risks and the pangs of exile. But there are probably more who, though they may be envious of America's plenty, are genuinely fearful of its military power and repelled by the social anarchy, the economic insecurity and inequality of which they have so often and relentlessly been told. Stories of unhappy returnees are made more credible by television documentaries that, as this viewer can testify, offer realistic, if carefully selected, images of the real ills of American society.

And in the sibylline utterances of Alexander Solzhenitsyn, echoes can again be heard of the philosophical and moral condemnation many Russian thinkers and writers have visited upon the materialistic West for a century and a half. In his "Letter to the Soviet Leaders" of 1973 as in his Harvard Commencement speech of 1978, America furnished examples of the freedom that "degenerates into complacency and licentiousness" and of "democracy run riot." Electoral contests in which, every four years, the politicians nearly kill themselves trying to gratify the masses; a president's performance judged by the voters' incomes or the availability of gasoline; a judge pandering to the passions of society and acquitting a defendant (Daniel Ellsberg) who during a difficult war steals and publishes Defense Department documents; mighty America losing to tiny North Vietnam because of a loss of nerve and a weak and undeveloped national consciousness; the uniformity of thought imposed by fashion and the media; commercial advertising, TV stupor, and intolerable music crowding out the longing for things higher, warmer, and purer.

There are telltale symptoms by which history gives warning to a threatened or perishing society. Such are, for instance, a decline of the arts or a lack of great statesmen. Indeed, sometimes the warnings are quite explicit and concrete. The center of your democracy and of your culture is left without electric power for a few hours only, and all of a sudden crowds of American citizens start looting and creating havoc. The smooth surface film must be very thin, then, the social system quite unstable and unhealthy.

Solzhenitsyn's evocation of America's demons is far removed, of course, in inspiration and intent from the uses Soviet propagandists have made of them. On the other hand, it is almost certain that no serious Soviet student of America would make a similarly superficial assessment of the resilience of its social fabric. The point, however, is not to show how far the passionate sincerity of the great dissenter may have carried him, much less to suggest a permanence or inevitability of negation. It is, rather, to emphasize that Russian and Soviet, official as well as unofficial, perceptions of America are made up, in shifting proportions, of affinities and contrasts, of memories of friendship and hostility, of realism and dogmatism, of bright and dark colors. Future generations, as have previous ones, will select those that need and preference, politics and prejudice dictate.[52]

NOTES

1. J. F. Loubat, *Narrative of the Mission to Russia in 1866 of the Hon. Gustavus Fox* (New York, 1873), and H. Rogger, "Russia and the Civil War," in Harold Hyman, ed., *Heard Round the World: The Impact of the Civil War Abroad* (New York, 1969), pp. 177–256.
2. M. P. Pogodin, "Letter on Russian History," in Hans Kohn,

ed., *The Mind of Modern Russia* (New Brunswick, 1955), pp. 60–68, and A. A. Woldman, *Lincoln and the Russians* (New York, 1961), pp. 241–50.

3. Fox to Charles Sumner, January 4, 1867 (Sumner Papers, Houghton Library, Harvard University, No. 26, Vol. 80).

4. A. I. Gertsen, *Sobranie sochinenii* (Moscow, 1954–1964), XIX, pp. 138, 141; A. A. Kraevskii, ed., *Piatiletie gazety "Golos"* (St. Petersburg, 1878), p. xxii.

5. M. N. Katkov, *Sobranie peredovykh statei "Moskovskikh vedomostei"* (Moscow, 1897), Vol. IV, 7–10, 339–341, 369–370, 424; VII, 9, 714 and T. C. Owen, *Capitalism and Politics in Russia* (Cambridge and New York, 1981), pp. 73–4, 104.

6. I. S. Aksakov, *Sochineniia* (Moscow, 1887), Vol. VII, 52–65.

7. Gertsen, *Sobranie sochinenii*, Vol. XIX, 139–40; XX, 87.

8. Robert Magidoff, "American Literature in Russia," *Saturday Review of Literature* (November 2, 1946), p. 9.

9. Rogger, "Russia," pp. 197–201, 248–250; David Hecht, *Russian Radicals Look to America, 1825–1894* (Cambridge, Mass., 1957), *passim*.

10. A. T. Beveridge, *The Russian Advance* (New York, 1904), p. 430; F. M. Dostoevskii, *Sobranie sochinenii* (Moscow, 1956), Vol. X, 146–56, 210.

11. V. G. Korolenko, *Puteshestvie v Ameriku* (Moscow, 1923), and *Sobranie sochinenii* (Moscow, 1956), Vol. X, 146–56, 210.

12. Maksim Gorkii, *Polnoe sobranie sochinenii* (Moscow, 1968–1976), Vol. VI, 194–273 and *The City of the Yellow Devil. Pamphlets, Articles and Letters About America* (Moscow, 1972).

13. W. F. Wilcox, ed., *International Migrations* (New York, 1931), Vol. II, 529; I. K. Okuntsov, *Russkaia emigratsiia v Severnoi i Iuzhnoi Amerike* (Buenos Aires, 1967), pp. 218–222; L. Krzhivitskii, "Za Atlanticheskom Okeanom," *Mir bozhii*, No. 1 (1896), p. 90.

14. For Russian reactions to the American Revolution and early America see M. M. Laserson, *The American Impact on Russia, 1784–1917* (New York, 1951) and two works by a leading Soviet historian which are available in American translations: N. N. Bolkhovitinov, *The Beginnings of Russian-American Relations, 1775–1815* (Cambridge, Mass., 1975) and *Russia and the American Revolution* (Tallahassee, Fl., 1976).

15. P. P. Svinin's *Opyt zhivopisnago puteshestviia po Severnoi*

Amerike (St. Petersburg, 1815, 1818) is available in an English version prepared by Avrahm Yarmolinsky, *Picturesque United States of America* (New York, 1930). P. I. Poletika's *A Sketch of the Internal Conditions of the United States of America and of Their Political Relations with Europe* (Baltimore, 1826) was never published in Russia. Only excerpts appeared in Russian journals.

16. A. B. Lakier, *Puteshestvie po Severo-Amerikanskim Shtatam, Kanade i ostrovu Kube*, 2 vols. (St. Petersburg, 1859) and *A Russian Looks at America. The Journey of Aleksandr Borisovich Lakier in 1857*, trans. and ed. A. Schrier and J. Story (Chicago, 1979); P. I. Ogorodnikov, *Ot N'iu-Iorka do San Frantsisko i obratno v Rossii* (St. Petersburg, 1872) and V *strane svobody* (St. Petersburg, 1882).

17. P. A. Tverskoi, *Ocherki Severo-Amerikanskikh Soedinennykh Shtatov* (St. Petersburg, 1895). Excerpts in Oscar Mandlin, ed., *This Was America* (Cambridge, Mass., 1949), pp. 349–70.

18. Tverskoi, "Pis'mo," *Russkaia mysl*, No. 5 (1910), p. 101.

19. G. F. Kennan, *Russia Leaves the War* (Princeton, 1956), p. 18; F. F. Schuman, *American Policy Toward Russia Since 1917* (New York, 1928), p. 45; U.S. Special Diplomatic Mission to Russia, *America's Message to Russia* (Boston, 1918), pp. 6, 42.

20. V. I. Lenin, *Polnoe sobranie sochinenii*, 5th ed. (Moscow, 1958–1965), Vol. XXXVV, 59, 83.

21. D. I. Mendeleev, *Raboty po selskomu khoziaistvu i lesovodstvu* (Moscow, 1954), 541; *Sochineniia* (Leningrad, 1937–1952), Vol. XX, 501; I. Kh. Ozerov, *Iz zhizni truda* (Moscow, 1904); *Chemu uchit nas Amerika?* (Moscow, 1908); *Novaia Rossiia* (Petrograd, 1916), pp. 73–87.

22. *Lenin on the United States* (New York, 1970), comp. C. Leiteizen from *Collected Works* (Moscow and London, 1963–1969), pp. 49–51, 60–61, 90–92, 97–99; F. C. Barghoorn, *The Soviet Image of the United States* (New York, 1950), p. 15.

23. V. V. Maiakovskii, *Polnoe sobranie sochinenii* (Moscow, 1955–1958), Vol. II, 113–164; VII, 20–95; 265–346; Charles Rougle, *Three Russians Consider America* (Stockholm, 1976), pp. 97–142; A. P. Reilly, *America in Contemporary Soviet Literature* (New York and London, 1971), pp. 12–22.

24. S. Frederick Starr, *Red and Hot. The Fate of Jazz in the Soviet Union, 1917–1980* (New York, 1983), pp. 62–78.

25. Albert Pinkevitch, *The New Education in the Soviet Republic* (New York, 1919), p. 163; Theodore Dreiser, *Dreiser*

Looks at Russia (New York, 1928), p. 52; Maurice Hindus, *Red Bread* (London and New York, 1931), p. 31.

26. H. V. Kaltenborn, *We Look at the World* (New York, 1930), p. 117; Hindus, *Humanity Uprooted* (New York, 1929), pp. 355–369, and *Broken Earth* (New York, 1931), pp. 29, 107, 169; I. V. Stalin, *Sochineniia* (Moscow, 1947), Vol. VI, 186–188.

27. K. E. Bailes, "The American Connection: Ideology and the Transfer of Technology to the Soviet Union, 1917–1941," *Comparative Studies in Society and History*, Vol. 23, No. 3 (July 1981), pp. 421–448.

28. Ibid., p. 444.

29. Valentin Kiparsky, *English and American Characters in Russian Fiction* (Berlin, 1964), pp. 134–141; Hans Rogger, "Amerikanizm and the Economic Development of Russia," *Comparative Studies in Society and History*, Vol. 23, No. 3 (July 1981), pp. 382–420.

30. Ilia Ilf and Evgenii Petrov, "Odnoetazhnaia Amerika," in *Sobranie sochinenii* (Moscow, 1961), pp. 7–448. English trans. Charles Malamuth, *Little Golden America* (New York, 1937).

31. Ilia Erenburg, "V Amerike," *Izvestiia*, July 16, 17, August 7, 1946; Barghoorn, *Soviet Image of the United States*, pp. 44–46.

32. G. F. Kennan, *Memoirs, 1925–1950* (New York, 1969), pp. 253–255.

33. Barghoorn, *Soviet Image of the United States*, p. 104.

34. *Politicheskii dnevnik, 1964–1970* (Amsterdam, 1972), p. 230; Starr, *Red and Hot*, pp. 215–16; H. E. Salisbury, *American in Russia* (New York, 1955), pp. 261–3; Alexander Solzhenitsyn, *The First Circle*, trans. T. P. Whitney (New York, 1968), p. 168.

35. Franklyn Griffiths, *Images, Politics, and Learning in Soviet Behavior Toward the United States* (Ann Arbor, Mich., 1976), 53ff.

36. L. A. Bagramov, *Chto ikh trevozhit?* (Moscow, 1960); S. M. Malyshev and V. S. Zorin, *SSSR i SShA dolzhny zhit v mire i druzhbe* (Moscow, 1959); Hans-Hermann Höhmann, *Züruck zu Chruschtschow? Zur sowjetischen Parole vom Einholen und Überholen der amerikanischen Wirtschaft* (Bonn: Bundesinstitut für ostwissenschaftliche und internationale Studien, December 1971); N. S. Khrushchev, *Khrushchev Remembers*, trans. and ed. Strobe Talbott (Boston and Toronto, 1974), p. 369.

37. N. N. Inozemtsev, "Sovremennye SShA i sovetskaia ameri-

kanistika," *SShA—ekonomika, politika, ideologiia,* No. 1 (1970), pp. 6–14; Nathan Leites, *The New Economic Togetherness: American and Soviet Reactions* (Santa Monica, Ca., December 1973); Stephen Gibert, *Soviet Images of America* (New York, 1977), p. 60.

38. *Pravda* and *Izvestiia,* March 10, 1963/*Current Digest of the Soviet Press,* March 27 and April 10, 1963; Starr, *Red and Hot,* pp. 269–275.

39. *Pravda* and *Izvestiia,* June 29, 1963/*Current Digest,* July 10, 1963. Nekrasov's account of his Italian and American trips was first published in the literary journal *Novyi Mir* in November and December 1962. A revised version appeared in his *Puteshestviia v raznykh izmereniiakh* (Moscow, 1967). References are to the American translation by E. Kulukundis, *Both Sides of the Ocean* (New York, 1964).

40. Khrushchev, *Khrushchev Remembers,* pp. 373–374.

41. Nekrasov, *Both Sides of the Ocean,* p. xii.

42. *Komsomolskaia Pravda,* January 20, 1963/*Current Digest,* February 27, 1963; *Izvestiia,* January 20, 1963/*Current Digest,* February 13, 1963.

43. Nekrasov, *Both Sides of the Ocean,* pp. 47, 95–7, 105–6, 141–44.

44. For this sampling I have made use of the *Current Digest of the Soviet Press* and of almost sixty books and brochures. I am grateful to Liuba F. Wong and Michael Gelb for the help they provided through UCLA's Committee on International and Comparative Studies.

45. *SShA,* No. 1 (1970)/*Current Digest,* March 24, 1970; *Pravda,* July 22, 1973/*Current Digest,* August 15, 1973; *Pravda,* April 2, 1976/*Current Digest,* April 28, 1976; *Pravda,* March 3, 1980/*Current Digest,* April 2, 1980.

46. *Izvestiia,* January 30, 1972/*Current Digest,* February 23, 1972. The article was written by N. N. Iakovlev, author of biographies of Franklin D. Roosevelt (Moscow, 1965 and 1981) and George Washington (Moscow, 1973).

47. Morton Schwartz, *Soviet Perceptions of the United States* (Berkeley and Los Angeles, 1978), 136.

48. *Pravda,* August 29, 1976/*Current Digest,* September 29, 1976; Maurice Friedberg, "The United States in the USSR," *Critical Inquiry,* Vol. II (Spring 1976), pp. 519–83; Starr, *Red and Hot,* pp. 303–20.

49. Robert Gillette, "The Soviet Union—At War with 'The Whole Dirty Wave,'" *Los Angeles Times,* July 29, 1984, "Calendar," p. 3; Friedberg, *loc. cit.,* Marianna Tax Choldin, "Censorship via Translation," Paper presented at the Ken-

nan Institute for Advanced Russian Studies, Wilson Center, March 1983.

50. *Izvestiia*, October 7, 1983/*Current Digest*, November 2, 1983.

51. *Izvestiia*, November 16, 1983/*Current Digest*, December 14, 1983; *Izvestiia*, March 21, 1984/*Current Digest*, April 18, 1984; *Pravda*, May 28, 1984/*Current Digest*, June 27, 1984.

52. A. I. Solzhenitsyn, *Letter to the Soviet Leaders*, trans. H. Sternberg (New York, 1974), pp. 46, 50–51 and *Alexander Solzhenitsyn Speaks to the West* (London, 1978), p. 91.

AFTERWORD

Mark Garrison

By the end of the first fifty years of U.S.-Soviet relations, nuclear weapons—which were not even invented when Roosevelt and Litvinov exchanged notes establishing relations in 1933—had become a central concern. Despite their centrality, however, they are often taken for granted as part of the background in discussing relations between the two countries. This afterword places the danger of mutual nuclear annihilation in the foreground as a source of illumination to throw into sharper relief key aspects of the relationship. This approach should not, indeed cannot, replace careful analysis of the relationship from more traditional perspectives. But perhaps it can provoke us into trying to understand how the two countries came to be poised near the brink of nuclear disaster and how they might be able to back away from it.

The premise of this approach—that nuclear weapons have become an active threat to the security of both countries—is not universally accepted. There is ambivalence among Americans about nuclear weapons: are they blessing or curse? Two weeks after the first atomic bomb was used in warfare in August 1945, *Time* magazine posed this question as a recognition that "the discovery which had done most to end the worst of wars might also, quite conceivably, end all wars—if only man could learn its control and use . . . The promise of good and evil bordered alike on the infinite." [1] Forty years later, some argue that indeed the bomb has been a good thing; it has prevented a war between the Soviet Union and the West, a war that might have been inevitable, in view of our deep differences, and would have caused immense destruction, particularly in Europe, even without nuclear weapons.

But American opinion seems to be moving away from that conclusion. Where a 1949 survey by Gallup showed that only 29 percent of Americans thought that the development of the atomic bomb was bad, and a 1954 survey found that 54 percent believed that the hydrogen bomb made another world war less likely, by 1982 65 percent of Americans had come to believe it was a "bad thing" that the atomic bomb was developed. [2] The American public has come to appreciate the watershed character of nuclear weapons for American policy. National surveys in the mid-eighties show that three out of four Americans believe that nuclear war cannot be kept limited and, if it occurred, would mean the complete destruction of both superpowers. The same proportion of Americans recognize that we cannot ever be sure that life on earth would continue after a nuclear war. [3]

The broad support for those two assumptions about nuclear war—that America most certainly would not survive and that we cannot be certain any human life would survive—have lent unprecedented intensity to the examination of the history of U.S.-Soviet relations for clues about the future, and in particular to the question: Can the past suggest avenues for avoiding nuclear con-

flict? The consequences are too final, too cataclysmic for
us to fail to try to prevent it. Even those who believe the
chances are slight that such a war will occur agree that
even a one in one hundred chance is too great a risk
and favor steps to reduce that risk. And the risk is put
much higher by large numbers of Americans, who make
an instinctive judgment based on the weapons amassed
and the deep differences and conflicts between the two
countries. If nothing else, a careful examination of U.S.-
Soviet relations over the past fifty years, indeed over the
past two centuries of Russian-American relations, can
help us understand why both the Soviet Union and the
United States have followed paths that led from a comfortable level of national security at the end of World
War II to the risk of annihilation.

American and Soviet leaders sensed the importance of
the two atomic bombs exploded on Japan in August 1945.
Looking to the future, Americans saw the bomb, in their
hands, as a means of assuring world peace forever. The
Soviet leaders, meanwhile, apparently viewed the acquisition of the atomic bomb as essential to their own security
and their role in the world. Why did both sides fail to
see where their policies would eventually lead? Or, to the
extent that they sensed what was coming, why did they
not act to head it off? Why did the two countries race
past so many cutoff points over the years, scarcely pausing
for reflection on the consequences for their future security? The answers lie in those factors of culture, history,
geography, ideology, and personality on which the contributors to this volume have drawn to weave the story
of U.S.-Soviet relations.

The American view of these weapons was formed in part
by our use of them to win the war against Japan. Plunged
into a war we did not seek, bloodied in a surprise attack,
we looked on the entire Japanese nation as our enemy
and saw no reason not to carry the war to the Japanese

people. Firebombing of cities established the principle, atomic bombs merely brought the latest technology to bear. Sure of moral superiority, we basked in total confidence in our ability to maintain technological supremacy over any other nation. Elimination of atomic weapons under international control was proposed in 1946 in the United Nations, but on terms not likely to have been acceptable to the Soviets even if they had been inclined to forgo the new weapons—which, by all indications, they were not. To the extent we anticipated the Soviets' developing their own atomic weapons, we assumed we could always maintain a technological edge so we would never be threatened.

This sense of superiority offered some comfort for Americans as the Cold War gathered momentum. Facing a Red Army in Europe that had not demobilized as we had, concerned by the decisive consolidation of Soviet control in Eastern Europe, anxious about communist inroads in Western Europe, we became still more concerned when Soviet manpower seemed to be augmented by hundreds of millions of Chinese under communist control. It was reassuring for Americans to think that if worse came to worst we could fall back on the bomb.

The Korean War should have given Americans pause. The atomic bomb did not prevent aggression nor forestall heavy American casualties once the decision had been made to resist aggression in the traditional way. Even when China entered the war and rolled back U.S. forces, the bomb was not used. Still there was faith in its efficacy; two years later, Eisenhower threatened to use it if the communist forces did not come to the truce table. They came, whatever the reason, which may have further encouraged Eisenhower and Dulles to rely on the threat of massive retaliation to keep the Soviets in line. But meanwhile the Soviet Union had tested an atomic bomb, then a hydrogen bomb, and was on its way to acquiring a complete nuclear arsenal. In due course that arsenal would call into question the American threat of nuclear retaliation, massive or otherwise, to prevent Soviet aggression.

But Americans did not face up to that reality. From the fifties to the eighties this reluctance to accept the meaning of nuclear weapons in Soviet hands was a blind spot in U.S. policy. The Soviet buildup in nuclear weapons eventually resulted in a standoff in which neither side could credibly threaten to initiate their use for any reason save as a last resort to preserve its existence. Instead we proceeded as though a succession of temporary advantages achieved through superior technology would enable us to use our nuclear weapons as leverage on Soviet behavior indefinitely. We allowed reliance on the nuclear threat as a deterrent of *nonnuclear* aggression to become so embedded in U.S. and NATO strategy that it impeded the buildup of Western nonnuclear defenses.

The reasons for this lack of vision relate to our history, our geographic isolation, and our political culture. Since the early nineteenth century, we had been able to isolate ourselves from the world's turmoil, except when we felt moved to emerge from our sanctuary and intervene for our own reasons and in a manner of our own choosing. Pearl Harbor was a shock, but the attack took place more than two thousand miles from San Francisco. Our sense that our homeland was secure from attack reduced our concern about retaliation for our firebombing attacks on German and Japanese cities; we could be confident that our enemies were unable to respond in kind on American soil. Faith in our technological superiority, in the rightness of any decision we might take to visit retribution on an enemy, and in our immunity from retaliation has been part of our basic makeup, bequeathed to us by geography and history.

The changes brought by a potential enemy's acquisition of nuclear weapons and the means to deliver them swiftly and surely on our homeland have therefore been difficult for Americans to assimilate. Along with other difficult lessons of the seventies—the failure in Vietnam, the Iranian hostage crisis, the larger sense of having lost the capability to work our will at great distances—our growing realization that our entire society is vulnerable presents a daunting psychological hurdle for all Americans. The comfortable world of the past is slipping from our grasp, and we cannot abide the thought.

An understanding of what disturbs us could be the first step toward dealing realistically with the problem of agreeing what national interests are truly vital and how to defend them without risking nuclear war. This necessarily must be a process of self-discovery. While it would be facilitated if our Soviet antagonists, out of their own self-interest, sought to understand our concerns and made efforts to avoid exacerbating them, in the past they have not demonstrated much inclination to do so.

As with Americans, one cannot understand Soviet attitudes without looking at the past. The record of Russia's slow rise to nationhood, repeated invasions and occupations by neighbors from almost every direction help explain Russian and Soviet preoccupation with security and the drive to enhance Russian security at the expense of the security of others by expanding. The ingrained sense of vulnerability is an important ingredient in Soviet behavior at home and abroad, in contrast to Americans' sense of invulnerability. Over the past fifty years, however, American and Soviet vulnerabilities have moved in opposite directions. When diplomatic relations were established in 1933, the U.S.—whatever its domestic problems—had reason to feel secure from any outside threat. The Soviet Union, on the contrary, could claim with some justice to feel encircled by potential enemies. Its weakness was illustrated by the unimpressive campaign against tiny Finland in the 1940 war and was brought home brutally by the ease with which Hitler swept to the gates of Leningrad, Moscow, and Stalingrad. Soviets know

how close they came to suffering the dismantlement of
the Soviet Union at Hitler's hands.

The trauma of World War II, however, became more
than just another invasion and another reason for seizing
territory to gain defense in depth. It was also a turning
point in Soviet self-esteem. The defeat of Nazi Germany
has come to be seen by Soviets as a nearly single-handed
achievement, at great sacrifice, by the peoples of the
Soviet Union, spearheaded by the Russians and led by
the Soviet government. In the process, honor was restored
to certain aspects of the cultural heritage of Russia—the
Orthodox Church and the reputations of certain tsars
were partially rehabilitated—thus further bolstering Russian self-esteem.

The victory also brought tangible fruits. The Soviet
Union acquired satellites and a significant role in the
postwar order. Its powerful land army and the territory it
controlled on its western borders greatly reduced its vulnerability to outside attack. It could consider itself more
secure from traditional invasion than at any time in Soviet or Russian history.

In the immediate postwar period, therefore, both the
U.S. and the U.S.S.R. had gained tremendously in terms
of prestige, power, and invulnerability, but the Soviets
had come the furthest. That being so, why did the Soviet Union not see that the greatest threat to its security
would come from atomic bombs and their even more
effective offspring? Armed with that vision, it might have
taken vigorous steps to ward off the threat. The most
extreme step would have been to trade off Soviet abstinence from the new weapon for the destruction of the
U.S. atomic arsenal, or holding it to a bare minimum,
under U.N. oversight. Perhaps American attitudes would
have caused the effort to fail, but why was no serious
effort made?

It is not necessary to look closely at peculiarly Soviet
motivations to recognize that self-denial does not come

naturally to leaders of major powers when contemplating powerful new instruments of war. The urge to acquire atomic weapons was, in any case, fed by every salient aspect of Stalin's political upbringing: reliance on force as the most important political instrument; bitter experience at the hands of a technologically superior enemy; and deep distrust of the intentions and latent perfidy of everyone, especially the leaders of "capitalist" countries. Stalin was hardly likely to rely on either the Americans' good faith or the effective oversight of an international organization. While abstinence from atomic weapons was clearly out of the question for the Soviet Union, there were other possible cutoff points in the arms race that would have made good sense in terms of long-range calculations of Soviet security. Why did the Soviets, like the Americans, fail to grasp such opportunities? The testing of hydrogen bombs, for example, could have been banned by mutual agreement and satisfactorily verified; this would have left both the U.S. and the Soviet Union in possession of atomic bombs, but the greatest threat to Soviet security would have been headed off. The testing of intercontinental missiles could have been banned. In later years, the Soviet Union could have exercised unilateral restraint in nuclear weapons, developing only enough to make sure the U.S. would never dare be the first to use them against the Soviet Union; unlike the U.S., which thought it needed nuclear superiority to hold back nonnuclear aggression by the Red Army, Moscow had no equivalent felt need to threaten first use of nuclear weapons: there was no massive conventional army poised on its western border.

In order to understand these failures of vision by Soviet leaders—the counterpart of failures on the American side—we need to consider, among other factors, the motivations that flow from the specific culture—Russian, Soviet, and Communist—from which Soviet leaders emerged. At the same time we must be aware of evolving attitudes and resist thinking of Soviet decision-makers merely as gray-faced Communist hierarchs uniformly cast from the same mold, unchanging from generation to generation. While they have much in common, one has only to cite the differences between Stalin, Khrushchev, and Brezhnev to underline the point.

Soviet policies of the late forties seem to have been guided by lessons and impulses of the past. Never again would the Soviet Union allow itself to be pushed to the wall by aggressors coming out of Western Europe. Eastern Europe was not merely a fruit of victory in a hard-fought war, it would also provide insurance against future aggression by keeping Germany permanently divided, with the Soviet-occupied part buffered by Soviet-controlled Poland and Czechoslovakia. This objective justified any skulduggery and any show of arms necessary to achieve it. The Red Army would show its strength to discourage aggression. On the other hand, if Tito could not be brought to heel, kick him out of the nest; Yugoslavia was not essential to Soviet security. The same was true of the Greek Communists: in terms of Stalin's cautious and conservative view of Soviet security, continued involvement was not worth the possible cost in view of Western reactions.

The long-term price for Stalin's efforts to consolidate the westward extension of Soviet frontiers was very high. Seen from the West, his actions were frightening. They led to the rearming of West Germany and the creation of NATO. And the perceived threat to Western Europe by a powerful Red Army gave rise to the U.S. threat to be the first to use atomic and nuclear weapons if it became necessary to stop Soviet aggression. This resolution contributed significantly to justifying the U.S. effort to maintain nuclear superiority through succeeding stages of the arms race.

Meanwhile, on the other side of the world, Stalin encouraged or ordered North Korean leaders to launch an attack on the South. The conventional wisdom is that he miscalculated, believing that the U.S. would consider

South Korea not worth fighting for, or if it did would be unable or unwilling to apply the force necessary to win. But it is not necessary to assume miscalculation on that score to show that Stalin was—in the East as well as the West—pursuing traditional advantages at the expense of the new calculations required by the advent of nuclear weapons. Stalin may have been looking somewhat further into the future. He may have foreseen that a unified, modernizing China could be a security threat to the U.S.S.R. even under Communist leadership, particularly if the U.S. supported China as it was beginning to help Tito's Yugoslavia. He might also have anticipated that a significant American military success in Korea would lead to a confrontation with China. But even if he were that prescient, Stalin's judgment still must be viewed as short-sighted. However desirable twenty years of hostility between China and the United States may have been from the Soviet point of view, the fact is that the Korean war strongly fed the feeling in the West that Soviet-inspired aggression was about to break out all over the world and that everything possible—including a buildup of atomic and nuclear weapons—must be done to deter it.

Stalin's policies thus relied heavily on calculations that were most appropriate to Russian and Soviet security concerns of the past and on outmoded ways of thinking about manipulating relations among states. His approach to atomic and nuclear weapons was probably influenced by the same old-fashioned thinking: if an enemy has a powerful weapon, so should I, and the more the better. It is also possible that Stalin was moved in part by another consideration, one that would become more noticeable in the attitudes of his successors: a feeling that with the victory over Hitler, the Soviet Union had arrived on the world scene as a major actor. No longer could the Soviet Union be ignored, ostracized, or dismissed. But if it wanted to assure its position as a world power, it must have the trappings. The Soviet role in the United Nations was one way of showing it had arrived; Soviet diplo-

matic activities, economic and military assistance, and
support of "progressive" movements in the Third World
was another; and Soviet military might—including the
newest atomic and nuclear weaponry—was perhaps most
important of all.

Stalin's successors seemed bolder in touting the Soviet
Union's position in the world. Not content with consoli-
dating an expanded empire, they exuded a new air of self-
confidence and looked to the future. Initially they even
aspired to overtake the U.S. in industrial production.
They would be more aggressive in cultivating friends and
clients all over the world and would support Communist
Cuba right under America's nose. In dealing with the
United States itself, they would insist on strict equality
as the other superpower. The Americans would have to
recognize that the "correlation of forces" had changed
and that the Soviet Union could no longer be trifled
with. This seemed to require, among other things, achieving at least parity in nuclear weaponry—not out of military necessity but to make a political point.

Thus, whether looking to the past, which meant looking
at nuclear weapons as though they were tanks (the more
the better), or to their future as a superpower with nuclear firepower at least equal to that of the United States,
Soviet leaders were inclined to favor an unrestrained
nuclear buildup. They were prepared, once they had
pulled even with the United States in nuclear striking
power, to agree to maintain rough equality. But they were
in no mood to bend over backward, to make concessions
just to get an agreement. They would insist on their own
definition of what constituted equality just as stubbornly
as the Americans insisted on theirs.

The same attitudes applied to the Soviet pursuit of
influence around the world. As a superpower, the Soviet
Union has claimed the right to pursue its interests wher-
ever and by whatever means it chooses: in Angola, the
Horn of Africa, the Middle East, Afghanistan, even in
America's hemisphere. If the Americans object, let them

find the means to make their objections effective. In the Soviet view, that is the way great powers in general and the U.S. in particular behave in the world. The Americans had it all for a while and have to face the reality that there is now another tough kid on the block.

We may dismiss this description of the Soviet state of mind as ethnocentric, overemphasizing the psychological effect on Soviet attitudes of having changed recently and rapidly from a weak power to a superpower. Whether or not the psychological aspect is exaggerated, we cannot ignore the fact that something has skewed Soviet priorities, with the result that Soviets have pursued gains that seem marginal to outsiders at the cost of risking their very existence.

American priorities can also be said to be skewed, with the same result: the absolute security from foreign threat which the United States enjoyed for 150 years has been dissipated through pursuit of imagined advantages made possible by nuclear weapons. American mistakes thus may be attributed to anxieties due to the gradual dissipation of the sense of omnipotence Americans enjoyed at the end of World War II. On the other hand, Soviet mistakes have been those of an insecure have-not nation that through its own sacrifices has achieved a precarious perch at the pinnacle of nations but is not satisfied that it has garnered either the psychic or the real fruits of that achievement.

Thanks to nuclear weapons, the destinies of two great nations have become inextricably entwined. If one perishes, so will the other. Each is a prisoner of the other's history and culture. For thirty-eight of the first fifty years of formal relations, we dealt with each other in the shadow of the bomb, but it cannot be said that we have brought increasing wisdom to the task. On the contrary, both sides have avoided facing up to the consequences of having created a machine which can destroy, quickly and completely, everything we value.

If our shared destiny is not to be oblivion, Americans

and Soviets will have to scrutinize history and the roots of our attitudes to understand the reasons for our mistakes. Then each people must find a way to surmount its history, culture, fears, and prejudices to arrive independently at the conclusion that there should be no higher priority than preventing a war that would end both societies and perhaps all human civilization.

NOTES

1. *Time*, August 20, 1945.
2. Daniel Yankelovich et al., eds., *Voter Options on Nuclear Arms Policy* (Washington, D.C.: The Public Agenda Foundation and the Center for Foreign Policy Development, 1984), p. 17.
3. Yankelovich, p. 24.

INDEX

Mark Garrison is director of the Center for Foreign Policy Development at Brown University.

Abbott Gleason is professor of history at Brown.

George Kennan is former United States Ambassador to the Soviet Union and author of 13 books on international affairs and politics. John Lewis Gaddis is professor of history at the University of Ohio. Adam B. Ulam is director of the Russian Research Center at Harvard University. Alexander Dallin is professor of history and political science at Stanford University. Robert Dallek and Hans Rogger are professors of history at UCLA.